Chad,
Become What
You Believe!

BROKEN ROAD

Turning My Mess
Into A Message

TONY COLLINS with Bethany Bradsher

ISBN-13: 978-1480025721
ISBN-10: 1480025720

Cover and interior design by Stephanie Whitlock Dicken.
Cover photo by Theo Parker.
Photos on pages 65, 126, 130 and 131 by Theo Parker.
All other photos courtesy of Tony Collins.

．．．

I dedicate this book to my wife, Trudy and to my mom and dad, Elizabeth and Calvin Collins.

．．．

INTRODUCTION

I believe that God doesn't give us things; He gives us opportunities. God has given me an opportunity to be raised by two great parents. He has given me an opportunity play on an undefeated high school football team my senior year, an opportunity to get a full scholarship to East Carolina University, an opportunity to get drafted by the New England Patriots in the second round, an opportunity to play in a Pro Bowl, an opportunity to play in Super Bowl XX, and now an opportunity to share my life with you. I also believe that every mistake we make, or as my wife would say, "choice," creates an opportunity—an opportunity to learn, an opportunity to get stronger, but most importantly an opportunity to help someone else. It doesn't matter how many mistakes we make; what matters is what we do with the opportunity. I believe that God will not only give you a second chance, but a third, fourth, fifth, sixth and seventh chance, as you will see in my life. Life is what we make it— what we think about the most will come to us. The problem is, what are we thinking about the most? I believe my life will help you change your way of thinking, because in order to see change on the outside, there must first be change on the inside. I thank God for the opportunities.

TONY COLLINS

CONTENTS

ACKNOWLEDGMENTS

FROM TONY:

Special thanks to my kids Nisi, Terrie, Colette, Conredge, TJ, Alisha, Paris, Toni, and Taylor and my grandkids Antonio, Angi, Baylor, Tyson, Jayden and the rest of my big family for always loving me no matter what! I would also like to thank the great town of Penn Yan, New York as well as all of my teachers, my coaches, my classmates and my teammates.

FROM BETHANY:

I'm grateful first to Tony for his incredible patience and enthusiasm through this project. Also special thanks to Lisa Stroud and Kit Sublett for editing help and guidance, and finally to my husband Sid and my children Preston, Holly, Ben and Jake for loving me, making me laugh and supporting me no matter what.

CHAPTER ONE

MY MESS

*It doesn't matter how many times you get knocked down—
what matters is that you get back up.*

I don't remember every detail about that awful morning in Indianapolis, but the guy in black is burned into my memory. I was on the grass outside my apartment complex, having convulsions, flopping up and down. There was this big wide field nearby, and I saw a man walking toward me, dressed in all black. I said to myself, "I don't want to die like this."

I was in terrible shape, even before I ended up shaking in the grass. I had been up for six days straight smoking crack cocaine, or freebasing, as we called it back in 1988. I wouldn't eat anything, because the drugs affected my appetite, and I was too wired on crack to sleep. The only thing I consumed, besides cocaine, was orange juice. One of the many girls I was with during that time in my life was at my apartment with me—I don't even remember her name.

That morning, I took a cocaine rock and put it on the table so that I could smoke it. Before my eyes, I swear, that rock jumped off the table, but when I looked on the floor I couldn't find it anywhere. I cooked up another rock and put it on the table and the same thing happened, and then the third one

1

jumped off the table too. At this point I was pretty sure I was losing it, so I went into the bathroom. When I looked in the mirror, my pupils were dilated—they were just huge—and my heart was beating really fast.

I woke up the girl and told her that I thought something was wrong with me. I drank some water and decided that what I really needed was some fresh air. When I got outside the building, my heart was just pounding so hard. "I think you need to call the ambulance," I told the girl. I was really afraid.

Right after that I started convulsing, and the girl ran inside to call 911. At the moment when I saw the mysterious man walking toward me, I was sure that I felt my spirit leaving my body, sure that I was getting ready to die. I was twenty-nine years old, I had played in the Super Bowl and the Pro Bowl for the New England Patriots, and I had once rushed for 1,049 yards and 10 touchdowns in a single season. And here, in this patch of grass, that big NFL dream and my singlehanded destruction of it were about to come to an end.

I cried out to God saying, "God, I do not want to die like this."

Suddenly, I lifted my head up, and the man in black was gone. My heart rate calmed down, and I felt OK. I actually got up and went inside, but my girlfriend had already called the ambulance. I hurried in to get rid of all of the drug stuff so that the paramedics wouldn't find it, and when they arrived they took my vital signs—which were still sky high—and took me to the hospital.

Later that day, it was all over ESPN and the papers in Indianapolis and New England: Tony Collins, once one of the most talented running backs in the NFL, was hospitalized following a drug overdose. Just months after being suspended from the league for one year for a series of failed drug tests,

I had plummeted from the top of the pro football mountain to something that looked a lot like rock bottom.

My family had to learn the depths of my addiction from those news reports. At that point, they realized how close I was to killing myself, and my brother Moose and my cousin Eddie decided to fly to Indianapolis to try to bring me home to New York. The doctors made me spend the night at the hospital, warning me to stay away from drugs because I had suffered a slight heart attack. The girl I was with took me home, and soon after that I went to the airport to pick up my brother and cousin. They were determined to talk some sense into me, or at least to get me in the car heading east so that they could keep me safe.

That crazy night when the ambulance took me away, I had asked one of my drug friends to hold onto my Super Bowl ring for me, so that it wouldn't disappear. So the day after Moose and Eddie arrived, we went out to eat breakfast and then I told them we needed to stop at my friend's house to pick up my ring. This guy was the only kind of friend I had at that time—a friend I got high with. We got to his house, and I left my brother and cousin in the car and went inside.

When I walked in the door, I realized that there was a group of people in there freebasing coke, and even after what I had gone through just days ago, I couldn't resist taking a hit. Of course, there was no such thing as just one hit. Everything I did at that stage, I did to an extreme. We were smoking, and after about thirty minutes or so, we heard a knock on the door. It was my brother and my cousin. I tried to tell them that I was negotiating with my friend, because he wanted to keep my ring, but then they walked in and realized what was really happening.

I was already high at that point, and there was no point trying to talk sense to me. I told them I was going to stay there until all the cocaine was gone, so I gave them the Super Bowl ring and they left and came back two hours later. They were really, really pissed off at me. They kept saying, "You know how many people love you? And you don't even care about yourself." Of course, at that point all of it was going in one ear and out the other.

When I look back on that day now, I can't believe it. How insane is that, when you just overdose two days earlier, to go right back to doing the same thing again? Just the thought of it is so crazy.

The next morning, when we got up, they tried again to get me in the car to drive back to New York. I told them that I didn't want to leave Indianapolis, which for some reason felt like home to me then, even though I had never made any connections there that weren't related to drugs. I had some money, and so I bought them both plane tickets back to New York, and they were gone. I can't imagine how their conversation went on the way back. I know I caused my loved ones an unbelievable amount of pain during that time.

Soon after they left, my mom called me and begged me to come home. I told her a bunch of lies—that I wasn't ready to leave yet, because I had some things I had to do in Indy. She said, "Son, just read the Bible. Start at Genesis." Later that night, after I had smoked some crack, I remembered what my mom said and I went and found a Bible I had there. I was high, but I was trying to do what my mom told me to do. But I couldn't even find Genesis.

Here I was, a man who had spent every Sunday of my life in church, and I was flipping through the New Testament, looking for Genesis. I think about that sometimes and I just can't get over it. My mind was so gone. Finally I looked at the very beginning of the Bible and I found it, and I started reading a little, then I got high some more. It was really a bad scene. I was out there by myself, and I had no one—only the progression of women who were around for a good time but really didn't care about me.

I had so many close calls during those months—one sign after another that God really intended to keep me around for a purpose. I stayed in Indianapolis for about another month, until I decided I needed to make some money to support my habit so I went to Chicago, where someone told me I could get drugs to sell. Another guy was riding with me, but I was driving my car with an expired license. Sure enough, we got pulled over, and I was really worried because of my license. On a whim, I took out a $100 bill and just put it at the window as the cop approached. Without saying anything, he took the money, walked back to his car and drove away.

Just a little while later, back in Indy, I had an even closer scrape with the law. I had driven my Jaguar to a rough apartment complex to buy some cocaine. As I was leaving, suddenly four or five unmarked police cars surrounded my car. My backseat was absolutely full of drug paraphernalia, not to mention about an ounce of cocaine. I could have been in prison for a long time if they just peeked in the window, but my windows were tinted really dark. The officers were trying to look into the car, but they couldn't see anything. Then one of them asked me if they could search my car.

I figured that was it—I was done. I was about to say yes, and then one of the other cops pulled me to the side—I guess he knew who I was—and told me in a low voice, "You know, you don't have to let us search your car." So I told them no, and they got in their cars and drove away. I didn't deserve protection with the way I was acting at that time, but I'm sure that God or angels or somebody was watching over me that night, because otherwise I was going straight to jail. My heart was beating so fast. You would think that the first thing I did after that episode was go home and get rid of all that drug stuff, but instead I went home and got high. That's how messed up my mind was.

I had yet one more close call around that time, and it was the scariest one of all because it could have ended the lives of both my son and me. My plan to sell drugs in Indianapolis had gone nowhere; I was using more drugs than I was selling, and I was running out of money. Also, I missed my kids, so I decided to get in my car and drive to North Carolina, where they were living with their mother. When I got there, my ex-wife was living with some guy and staying high even more than I was. Our kids were two and four years old, and both of their parents were addicted to cocaine, more concerned with getting our drugs than with caring for our children.

The Jaguar I was driving was less than three years old, and I decided to trade it in on an older Jaguar so that I could get some money out of it. I got $12,000 on the trade, and I cashed the check and put all of that money in a bag. The next morning, after staying up all night doing drugs with my wife, I had to go back to the dealership to get the tags for my car, and my two-year-old son Conredge wanted to come with me. I was pretty out of it—I put him in the front seat with no car seat, no seatbelt, nothing. It was a short drive down I-85, and I remember seeing the sign that said my exit was one mile away.

The next thing I knew, I heard the sounds of metal hitting metal and my son crying, because he had been thrown down into the floorboard of the car. I had fallen fast asleep at the wheel, and the only thing that woke me up was the fact that my car ran into a car right in front of me. I pulled over, because I thought I would have to talk to the guy I ran into, but the other car just took off. Then I saw something that scared me to death.

I looked for my exit sign, and it was behind us! I had gone past the exit, fast asleep, which means I had been driving that way for more than a mile. It was a miracle. My car stayed in the lane, without getting in a major wreck, and then ran into another car just enough to wake me up, but not hard enough to hurt Conredge. If that isn't God, I don't know that there is a God. That was unbelievable, the way He protected us that day.

There is one more part of that story that actually makes me laugh. We finally got to the car dealership, and I was carrying the black bag full of $12,000 cash. We sat down in the waiting room while they prepared my tags, and I fell fast asleep again. When I woke up, Conredge had opened the bag and was playing with the money. There was cash spread out on the floor all over the room, and he was having a great time playing with all those bills. It's a wonder that someone didn't rob me blind.

Those few months, from October when I saw the man in black clothes to the next January when I fell asleep on the highway, were probably the darkest months of my life. There were plenty of trials still ahead, but I have never had so many close calls and near-death experiences in such a short time. I was still so gripped by my drug addiction and so focused on myself that I couldn't really see the reality that is crystal clear to me now: God had a purpose for my life and he was sparing me, even though I was trying as hard as I could to self-destruct.

For the last eight years, before my bad choices led to my suspension, I had been living my lifelong dream of playing football in the NFL. I had scored touchdowns in major games at both the collegiate and professional level and my name was easy to find in the Patriots record books. I had a loving family that had done all they could to sow seeds of responsibility and discipline into me, but during those few months in 1988 and 1989 I proved that I was operating entirely on my own and that I was more concerned with finding a quick high or a one-night stand than I was with values like family, friendship, diligence or self-control.

My downward spiral of poor choices had started innocently enough—with a few painkillers from team trainers who wanted to keep me on the football field even if I was injured. Just a few short years after I agreed to those first shots, I was drowning in a world of drugs and women and acting so self-absorbed that my family would have been justified in cutting me off completely. Like all addicts, I couldn't see past my quest for the next high.

On the sidewalk. At the traffic stop. On the highway. All three times it should have been over for me, but forces intervened that let me continue through life in safety. Of course, I am convinced that God was my lifeguard—that he tossed me life preservers in a variety of forms so that I could one day proclaim to anyone who would listen that God is in control. Today I want people around me, especially if they have been discouraged by life, to know that God doesn't give up on us. I want them to know that he loves to give second (and third and fourth) chances and that he can construct a redemptive masterpiece even from a broken life like mine.

• • •

CHAPTER TWO

PENN YAN

What you think about the most will come to you.

.

Through the twelve years I spent playing football on the collegiate and professional levels, I encountered plenty of teammates who had rough pasts—broken families, abuse, racism, addiction, all kinds of stuff. When I think about my own childhood, I realize that I didn't experience any of those things that would seem to predict trouble later in life. It was only as an adult that I saw how much I had to be thankful for.

I was the fifteenth of sixteen kids, and my parents raised my older brothers and sisters in their hometown of Sanford, Florida. But when I was only five months old they moved to upstate New York, to a small town called Penn Yan. My parents moved us such a long way because my aunt and uncle had come to Penn Yan a year earlier and they told my dad that he could find work there. It was a good place for him—eventually he even started his own construction business in Penn Yan.

There were no black people in Penn Yan except my six cousins, my aunt and uncle and my big family. Five of my older siblings were out on their own, so when we got to town we had ten kids from my family and my six cousins, and for a while we all slept under the same roof. I'm sure we made quite an impression on that little town.

Even though my family stood out like a sore thumb, we were treated well in Penn Yan. From a young age, I heard my parents tell stories of the racism they were subjected to growing up in Florida—rocks thrown at them as they walked to school, segregation limiting where they could go and which buses they could ride on. The only hint of that I experienced, later in my childhood, was when my white friends would come play at my house but never seemed to want to invite me to theirs. But for the most part, we were treated kindly, I think partly because Penn Yan was a football town and the Collins family turned out a lot of athletes. With one football player after another coming through the high school, we made their town better.

At times there were three or more of us sleeping in one bed, and I guess we were poor, but I never knew that. My childhood was just so much fun. There was always something to do, always someone to play with. I had one younger brother, but I still felt like the baby in the family, especially when my older brothers picked on me.

One of the important influences when I was young was church—we never missed a Sunday. There were black people in a nearby town called Geneva, and we drove there every Sunday to go to a black Baptist church. My father was a Sunday school teacher and a deacon, and my mom was in every group in the church. Geneva was twenty-five minutes away, and my dad had to be there by 8:30 to prepare to teach his lesson, so we had to get the whole family ready and out of the house early.

After Sunday school, we would have maybe a fifteen-minute break before the service, which would last two-and-a-half hours. We wouldn't finish that until one thirty, and we couldn't go home then because there was another service at three thirty. By the time we finished the second service and got home it was nighttime. Every Sunday, that's what we would do. All of us boys hated it, because back then the only televised NFL games were on at one and four, and by the time we came home all of the football would be over.

The other major influence for my brothers and me, and the thing that meant the most to us when we were young, was sports. Everybody loved sports, and we played all kinds—football, baseball, basketball, wrestling. We had this long backyard, which we needed, because we were always out there playing something.

My dad, Calvin Collins, played baseball in the Negro Leagues. They called him Big Pitch. Baseball was his favorite sport, and he wanted us all to play, but football was our main thing. Penn Yan was such a small town—only two red lights, and we didn't even get a McDonald's until I was in high school. But one thing that was big in Penn Yan was football.

All of my brothers were good athletes, but the one I looked up to the most was Morris, whom everybody called Moose. Moose was seven years older than me, and he was like Jim Brown—good at everything. He was one of the best football players Penn Yan had ever seen. As a junior high player, the coaches wouldn't let him run the ball because they thought he would run over the other kids and hurt them.

When Moose went out for the football team at Penn Yan Academy as a freshman, he made the varsity and became a starter. That had never happened to a freshman in Penn Yan before. So my whole thing, at that point in my life, was to be like Moose. He was my idol.

I decided that I was going to make the varsity as a freshman, just like Moose. I went to all of his games, and I tried to make it to all of his practices too, just to watch him. He had a tremendous impact on me. Moose would always talk about how he was going to play in the NFL, and pretty soon, even though I was only eight or nine, I started to say, "I'm going to play in the NFL, too."

I was just sure that Moose was going to be a big-time college player, but instead he went and played ball at a nearby community college, which was a disappointment to me. Later I found out that he got a girl pregnant and wanted to stay close to home. He did great there, but he never fulfilled that dream of making it to the NFL. I think that made me want it even more for myself.

Pretty soon playing in the NFL was all I thought about. I truly believe that there is power in our words and in our thoughts. I like to say that what you think about the most will come to you, and that everything begins with a thought. My single-minded approach to football during my childhood is evidence of that.

I was absolutely consumed with playing in the NFL. I remember many times when me and my brothers and cousins would be playing in our backyard and eventually everybody else would leave. But not me. I would stay out there by myself, making moves, pretending to run plays, hearing the roar of the NFL crowd in my head. If it was cold or rainy and I had to be inside, I would spend hours playing with my favorite toy, an electronic football game I got for Christmas one year. I spent so much time playing with that thing that my mom would have to come in and unplug it to force me to do my homework or go to bed.

My NFL dreams even affected my sleep patterns. I didn't need to get up until about seven when I was a kid, but I regularly woke up at five and couldn't get back asleep, because my mind was busy with thoughts of myself on a professional football field, wearing a big-time jersey, scoring touchdowns before the home crowd, playing in the Super Bowl or the Pro Bowl. It was all I thought about, every day.

When I was about eleven years old, I heard about the registration for Pop Warner football, and I was so excited. I signed myself up, but my heart sank to my feet when I saw the game schedule—all Pop Warner games were played on Sundays. I went home, waited for a good time to talk to my dad, and went to ask him for permission to miss church to play football. I was so nervous walking in to talk to him that day. I just knew that he was going to say no.

To my complete surprise, my dad agreed to let me and my younger brother Lloyd play. The rest of the family would leave early for church like always on Sundays, but we stayed home. When it was time to go to the game, we rode our bikes to the field, played in the game and then returned home and watched football on TV while we waited for them to come home.

I remember, in my very first Pop Warner game, I scored five touchdowns. I couldn't wait to tell my brothers and my dad when they came in from church. I always did well in those games, almost always scoring touchdowns. But as long as the games were on Sundays, my mom and dad never came and watched us.

I was such a fanatic about football, and it drove me crazy that my little brother didn't care about the sport as much as I did. One Wednesday evening our parents left for a prayer meeting and we were supposed to ride our bikes to practice.

After Mom and Dad left, Lloyd said that he wasn't going to go. I was so mad that I actually beat him up, and then I forced him to get on the handlebars of my bike to go to practice. He was crying, and things got worse when we hit a big bump and he fell off and hurt himself. I got in big trouble for that episode, and it was all because I thought everyone should share my passion for the game.

Later in my career, when I played on Fridays or Saturdays, my parents watched me play and always supported me, but I remember, during those Pop Warner years, feeling sad that my dad didn't want to come to my games. I didn't really understand at the time how fortunate I was to have a father who put God first in everything he did and wanted to pass that strong faith down to us. As I look back on it now, I see how powerful his example was.

I work with teenagers today, and so many of them don't have any kind of father figure in their lives. I consider myself blessed, even if Dad was hard on me at times. I was never afraid of my father, but I was afraid of disappointing him. He and my mom would both give us whuppings when we disobeyed. They would send us out in the yard to get our own switch, and then they would spank us with it.

One particular whupping, from the hands of my mom, really stands out in my mind. We didn't have the money to buy clothes, but my mom could sew, and she would make us these knit pants to wear to school. But I hated the knit pants, because all of my friends were wearing jeans, and I had taken to begging my parents to buy me a pair of jeans.

It was a school morning, and my mom got the homemade pants and told me to put them on for school. I asked again for a pair of jeans, and I was really frustrated when she said no.

So when my mom left the room, I grabbed a pair of scissors and cut the cord to her sewing machine. I must have been insane for a second.

All that day at school I could only think of one thing—how mom was going to kill me when I got home. On the way home on the school bus with my sister Sybil, she kept telling me how bad it was going to be for me. When I got home, mom was waiting with the sewing machine cord I had cut. She beat me with that cord until my rear end burned.

For the most part, though, I was a good kid. My younger brother got spanked a lot more than I did. I stayed out of trouble because I spent so much time playing football. Even when I got into high school, and a lot of my friends would drink beer, I stayed away from that kind of stuff. I tasted it once and thought it was nasty, and I knew that drinking and partying would keep me from reaching my NFL goal. I had also been raised to believe, as the Bible said, that my body was a temple of the Holy Spirit, and I needed to keep it pure.

I believed in God and in the Bible, not just because my dad wanted me to, but also because I wanted that faith for myself. I believed the scripture that said all things are possible with God, and so I believed that God could get me to the NFL. But I also grew up hearing something else: "Faith without works is dead." From that, I concluded that God was not going to lead me to my professional football dream without plenty of hard work on my part.

As high school approached, I was completely fixated on the Penn Yan Academy football tryouts. My brother Moose used to say, "Anthony, don't just be like me—be better than me." Of course, the first step on the road to that goal was making the varsity as a freshman, just like Moose had.

In that summer before the ninth grade, I worked out all the time. I would run stadium steps, do push-ups every night, the whole works.

When tryouts came, I played my best, but when I got there I realized there were some good upperclassmen running backs and the competition would be tough. I still believed that I could make the varsity, that goal I had set my sights on so many years earlier. They posted the team lists, and I didn't even look at the JV—I went straight to the varsity roster. My name wasn't there. I went home and I cried. When my name wasn't on that list, it was devastating to me. I knew I was good, but I thought I might not be good enough.

I remember that day so well. I went home in tears and told my mom that I had failed to make the varsity. She said, "Well, you made the JV team, that's good." She told me that all I could do was play my best on JV and try again next year. She reminded me that I had been given an opportunity to play JV, and I needed to take advantage of that opportunity. When my dad came home, I cried again. I thought they were going to be disappointed in me, but they never showed anything but love and support.

I did work hard as a JV player, even though I never really felt like I belonged on that team. I scored at least 15 touchdowns that season, and in the final game of the season, when they traditionally brought up a couple of the JV players to play on the varsity, I was chosen and finally got my chance.

I played a lot of downs for the Penn Yan varsity over the next three years. We were a small 1A school, but everyone in New York knew Penn Yan Academy for its strong football program. My sophomore year was disappointing—I missed half of the season with a broken wrist, I only scored seven touchdowns and the team had a mediocre record. After that setback, I changed my focus from my own football accomplishments to inspiring my team. As a junior, I was a team leader, and I encouraged all of my teammates to run stadium steps with me. We only had two losses that season.

Things really came together my senior year. We were killing 3A and 4A teams on a regular basis, and we ended the season as only the third undefeated squad in Penn Yan history, capping it off with the New York Class B State Championship. In my high school career, I scored 28 touchdowns and my friend and teammate Cris Crissy scored 29. That put us second and third in the Penn Yan record book behind my brother Moose, who had scored 36.

Cris Crissy was a wide receiver and a safety, and he was probably a more talented player than me. He would make the most unbelievable catches, and he made me better, because I wanted to be the best on the team. Cris never talked about playing in the NFL, but I remember one day at practice during our senior year I said, "Wouldn't it be really cool if both of us made it to the NFL?" I'm not sure if he even heard me, and here we were in this tiny town. I'm sure if he had heard me he would have thought I was crazy.

Fast forward four years, to NFL Draft Day in 1981. Cris had played wide receiver for Princeton and had a great career there, and I was successful at East Carolina. With their second pick, the New England Patriots selected me. With their twelfth pick, they chose Cris Crissy. He got cut in the preseason and was later picked up by the Washington Redskins, but I have always been amazed by the way our paths crossed again, not too far from upstate New York. To me, that story is another example of just how powerful your words can be.

High school was a great experience for me—I was successful as a football player, my parents continued to guide and encourage me and I always had plenty of brothers and friends to hang out with. As far as I was concerned, I had it all. I didn't even know we were poor until I went to college. I remember getting a five-speed bike in junior high. Everybody else already had one, but when I finally got one that was the coolest thing to me.

Everybody in Penn Yan knew who I was. When I was walking down the street people would say, "Hey Anthony." I didn't hang out with a whole lot of different kids, but I did have a few good friends. My best friend was a football teammate named Tom Watkins. We were like salt and pepper—every time you saw Tom, you would see me. He still comes up to Penn Yan to play in my charity golf tournament every year.

There were so many steady, loving people who pointed me in the right direction during my upbringing in Penn Yan. I am better because I grew up in a town that embraced and guided me, and I am especially grateful to people like Tom Watkins, Mr. and Mrs. Watkins, Cris Crissy, Tom Walker, Terry McMichael, Rich Enos, Coach Miner, Coach Brewer, Coach Smart, Coach Manley, Coach LaRock and Coach Noteware.

My dad was a rock for me through those years. I knew that he really loved baseball and wanted me to play, so as a freshman I played on the JV baseball team. But baseball was starting to get boring to me, and I wanted to run track instead, because I thought it would help me in football.

I remember I was so scared to tell him that I wasn't going out for baseball. I didn't say anything until he came to me and asked me when baseball practice was starting. But when I finally told him, he supported me even though I'm sure he was disappointed. And the coolest thing was, he didn't miss one football game during those years, no matter how far away we played. If the games were on Friday or Saturday, he would make sure he was there. There's no better feeling as a player than seeing your parents in the stands.

I was focused on helping Penn Yan to that state title as a senior, but college football was never too far from my mind. As I saw it, playing for a big Division I program wasn't the goal itself, but a crucial stepping stone on the way to the NFL. Syracuse was one of the first big programs to come around, and that school was interesting to me because it was only forty-five minutes away from home. I took my first official visit there, and I really liked it.

Before long, another good option presented itself. My dad had an uncle who worked in the athletic department at the University of Florida, and he convinced the Florida coaches to look at me. I flew down there for an official visit; it was my first time ever on a plane. I was unsure about Florida, because I thought it was a million miles from home, but when I went down there I fell in love with it. The athletic dorms were actually inside the football stadium, and I thought that was amazing, and it was so much warmer than upstate New York. After that visit, Florida was my first choice and Syracuse my second.

Then I got a phone call from a coach at a place called East Carolina University. It was a Division I school, but I had never even heard of it. I listened when the coach talked, but I certainly didn't think an unknown school could overshadow the University of Florida for me. Before I knew it, an ECU assistant coach showed up in Penn Yan. That impressed me —Syracuse and Florida hadn't sent coaches to see me—and I agreed to go to Greenville, North Carolina for an official visit.

When I made that trip, I still wasn't thinking about going to East Carolina, but soon I met the head coach, a guy named Pat Dye. Coach Dye told me that I would have a great future at ECU and that I would have plenty of opportunities to play there.

I was a little uneasy before I arrived, because of my older brothers. Before my visit, they kept telling me the same thing: "Watch out for rednecks!" I had no idea what they were talking about. I had never heard that term, and I just figured that when I got there I was going to see threatening people with bright red necks.

The ECU coaches took me to a famous local restaurant called Parker's, and they said we were going to eat barbecue there. In the North, where I grew up, barbecue meant cooking something on the grill, so I was taken aback when they brought me a plate of this strange ground-up meat. I wasn't that impressed with that meal, or with the party that one of the Pirate players took me to while I was there.

I was really naïve, a small-town boy, and I just wasn't into the party scene. I had dated some girls, but I didn't know how to dance and I was scared to approach a girl to ask her to dance. I also didn't know how to talk to black girls, because I had never been around them much. Most of the girlfriends I had in Penn Yan, like most of my friends, were white. People at the party were also drinking beer, and I was still sure that I didn't want any part of that.

So I wasn't entirely comfortable in Greenville, but I just fell in love with Pat Dye. He didn't say anything profound to me, but sometimes you just feel something special about a person. When I talked to Coach Dye, I just knew that East Carolina was the right school for me.

On the trip home from North Carolina, I was nervous about seeing my family. Once again I was about to tell my father something he probably wouldn't understand. Once again I was afraid that my parents and my brothers would be disappointed in me. They were really excited about the prospect of me playing football for the Florida Gators. When I got back to Penn Yan, we sat down to eat dinner, and they asked me how the visit went.

I remember most of my brothers were there, and of course my parents. I took a deep breath and said, "I don't think I want to go to the University of Florida anymore. I want to play for East Carolina." They asked me if I was crazy. My dad couldn't believe I would choose ECU over Florida, and I tried my best to explain the feeling I had about the coach and the program. I remember my father said, "I've heard of North Carolina, and I've heard of South Carolina, but where the hell is East Carolina?"

They didn't understand it at all when I first broke the news, but over time they accepted my decision. I was still nervous about the rednecks, whatever they were, that might be waiting for me in my new home. But when I got to the Deep South, it didn't take long for me to encounter some authentic rednecks on my new football team.

. . .

CHAPTER THREE

EAST CAROLINA

God doesn't give us things; He gives us opportunities.

I was pretty nervous about my move to North Carolina because of my close relationship with my family. It would be the first time I had ever lived away from home, and Penn Yan was eleven hours away. But my parents and siblings had no idea that I wasn't actually planning on going to college alone.

When I was a senior in high school, my parents finally saved up enough money to buy me a little car, and I used that freedom to drive to Geneva, the town where my church was. I met a girl there—my first black girlfriend—and soon we were in love. The summer after I graduated, she told me she was pregnant. I remember discussing abortion with her, but for me that really wasn't an option. And the one thing I knew was that I was not going to stay in Penn Yan.

I knew the right thing to do—stay with this girl and be a father to the baby. And I did love her, but I wasn't about to do what Moose had done and sacrifice my NFL dream. So she and I secretly began to plot about going down south together. There were a lot of vineyards in that part of New York, and you could make extra money by picking grapes, so my girlfriend and I started doing that to save up for our move.

In early August, a couple of weeks before I was scheduled to report to East Carolina, we loaded up the car, drove to Greenville and checked into a hotel, and our family still had no idea what we were up to. Finally, when we got there, we called home and I told my mom and dad where we were and that we were OK. My mom started crying, and my dad didn't say anything at all to me. I think he was really disappointed that we left the way we did.

It only took a day or two for us to realize that we had made a mistake. We had no plan at all. We didn't know where we were going to live, and because of football I couldn't work to make money for rent. It's not like I could move my girlfriend into the athletic dorm. I thought I was doing the right thing, but the best thing for her was to be at home with her family, and I wasn't about to deviate from my plan to play Division I football. So we drove all the way back to upstate New York.

My second trip to begin my collegiate life was a little more traditional. My parents and some of my brothers drove me down—there were so many of us that we needed two cars. When we arrived, my family helped me get moved into the dorm and then my parents bought me a bike to use around campus.

When they left for the long drive north, I was so lonely that I cried in secret for a couple of days. I met some of my teammates when preseason training camp started, but that didn't really help me feel like I belonged. I also got my first lesson in what a redneck really was.

I was walking out to the field by myself, and a couple of the Pirate players walked by. One of them, a white 300-pound lineman named Wayne Bolt, glanced at me and said, "Oh, we've got another coon on the team." I couldn't believe what I was hearing. Later, when I told one of my other teammates about the remark, he said, "Oh, that guy is a redneck." But when we started playing together, Wayne and I got along fine.

I had never lived in the South before, and I felt like a fish out of water for those first few months. The food was different, I wasn't used to the way people talked and the heat and humidity were terrible. Our first couple of days out on the field, in August in Eastern North Carolina, were almost unbearable for me. But I was determined to suck it up and work hard and not let my new teammates know that I was about to throw up. There were times I was sure I was about to be sick, but I held it back.

The guys on the team would also tease me about coming from New York: "You can't play no football if you're from New York." When they riled me, it made me even more focused on my goal and strengthened my work ethic on the football field. I was put on the active roster as a freshman, so the coaches thought enough of my potential to decide against redshirting me, but I played mostly on special teams and didn't get that many minutes, carrying the ball 21 times for 100 yards that season.

But even if I wasn't a star on the field yet, I was learning so much from my coaches and teammates. Eddie Hicks, a running back who went on to play two seasons for the Giants, was my greatest mentor my freshman year. ECU ran the wishbone offense, and I had no experience with that scheme, so I had to learn how to block the right way, and I even got to catch some passes in the wishbone. I kept my intensity dialed way up all the time in practice, because I wanted people to take notice.

On Monday and Tuesday of every week during the season, benchwarmers like me had to play on the scout team, trying to give the first-team defense a good look at what they would face on the upcoming Saturday. But I was more concerned with getting better than with giving them a good look, so I would bust the starting defenders, sometimes for 20 or 30 yards.

One linebacker, Harold Randolph, would get so mad when I would beat him as part of the scout team. When I saw Harold coming down the hallway of Belk Dorm, I would duck out of the way. He would try to take my head off in practice. But he made me better. I'm convinced that if I hadn't endured some of those hardships my freshman year I wouldn't have become the player I was later.

I respected my head coach Pat Dye so much, and one of the best things that happened to me as a freshman was that spring on Pro Day, when NFL scouts came to see our East Carolina seniors. I was out there watching the older guys strut their stuff, and Pat Dye pulled me over and told a couple of the scouts, "This guy right here, he's going to be an NFL player. You keep an eye on him." Of course, that was all I needed to hear to work even harder in the weight room and on the field.

Unfortunately, that work ethic did not extend to the classroom. My only purpose in going to college was to take the necessary steps toward the NFL, so I really didn't care about the academic side of things. I had never developed the discipline of studying, and football players didn't have mandatory study halls back then. I loved the freedom of living on my own, especially when it came to skipping class. If it was raining, or if it was cold outside, I wouldn't go to class.

Sometimes I would be on my way to class when I would see a girl and start talking to her. If she didn't have a class, suddenly I didn't have one either. I was still staying away from alcohol and drugs, but my freshman year in college was when I really started to become a womanizer. There were beautiful black women everywhere, and they would pay attention to the football players. I didn't have a girlfriend—and I was a long way from New York, where my first daughter Nisi was born that March—but I really liked spending time with pretty girls.

It's strange that I became so hooked on the company of women, because I was really kind of shy. During those college years, girls would approach me, but I would never strike up a conversation myself. They were taking the initiative, I guess partly because I was a football player. It was really too easy.

The result of such an undisciplined lifestyle? I finished my freshman year with a 0.7 grade-point average. Academic standards for student-athletes weren't as strict in the late seventies as they are today, but even then a 0.7 was not going to put you on the football field in the fall. So that spring Coach Dye called me into his office and told me that I wasn't going home to New York for the summer like I thought. I was enrolled in summer school at ECU.

Someone in the athletic department chose my summer classes for me, and they were incredibly easy. I took tennis and badminton and all kinds of other cake courses that required little or no effort. I did go to class—I had learned my lesson about that—and by the end of both summer sessions I had elevated my GPA to a 2.9. I didn't really improve my study habits, but my grades were good enough to stay on the football team, so I was happy.

My sophomore year presented new opportunities on the gridiron and also deeper friendships with other guys who stayed away from the party scene. I worked so hard that I became a starter at running back, and I had a great connection with our quarterback Leander Green, a talented guy who would have certainly played professionally if he had been bigger. I was comfortable with the wishbone, and I finished the year with 506 total rushing yards on 82 carries and 398 yards on kickoff returns.

Our Pirates squad was so successful that season—we finished with a 9-3 record and won our last four regular season games—that we qualified for ECU's first bowl in thirteen years. We were invited to face Louisiana Tech in the Independence Bowl, and we proved that we had earned our way onto that national stage by defeating the Bulldogs 35-13. I rushed for two touchdowns in that bowl game.

My buddies on the team were Tim Roach, Eric Dawson and Mike Hawkins. Tim and Eric had come to ECU to play football, but they were kept out that year by injuries. Mike was a running back like me, and that wasn't the only thing we had in common. He came from a family of twenty-one kids.

The four of us loved to go to parties, but none of us would drink or do drugs. Instead, we would see how many girls' phone numbers each of us could get when we were out together. None of us had much money, but we would pool our resources and walk up the hill from the dorm to Krispy Kreme to get a box of donuts and some milk. Then we would walk around, eating our donuts and looking for girls.

When we passed by Belk Hall, where the football players lived, we could smell marijuana smoke, and we knew guys were getting high inside. It was only later that we learned they were into much heavier stuff too—cocaine and LSD. With my friends by my side, I found it easy to resist at that point in my life. I still believed that my body was a temple and it was a sin to put anything bad into it. And I thought those guys were crazy for jeopardizing their football success in exchange for a quick high.

I had a different kind of reputation as an ECU Pirate—as the first one on the field and the last one off, the guy who would run stadium steps regularly just because he felt like he wasn't working hard enough. I was a fanatic in the weight room, squatting 650 pounds. And all of that focus and effort truly paid off when my junior season rolled around.

During that 1979 season, the college football world really began to take notice of Anthony Collins. In the wishbone, all we did was run the ball, so when I became the primary go-to guy as a junior my stats were ridiculous. I led the nation in three categories—total rushing, total scoring and average yards per carry (7.4 yards). I finished the season as ECU's leading rusher, with 1,150 yards on 154 attempts. Because the wishbone featured three backs I only carried the ball 15 to 20 times a game, but I made the most of those opportunities. I was named first team All-South Independent for my efforts that year.

My team continued to excel as well—we finished the season 7-3-1 to keep alive Coach Dye's streak of winning seven or more games in every one of his six ECU seasons. But our habit of putting together winning seasons meant that the college football community finally realized what those of us in Greenville already knew about Pat Dye—he was an exceptional coach. When the season was over, Dye was courted by several other Division I programs, and he accepted a job at Wyoming.

Coach Dye only stayed at Wyoming for one season before he landed his dream job at Auburn, the position that ultimately sent him to the College Football Hall of Fame.

In his twelve seasons at Auburn, Dye won 71.1 percent of the time and led the Tigers to nine straight bowl games. I was one of many players Coach Dye inspired throughout his impressive career. We still keep in touch today.

When I first heard the announcement that Coach Dye was leaving ECU, I was in denial. I only had one more year, and I was already starting to hear from pro scouts and agents. I really didn't understand the business side of it at that point; I just felt abandoned by the coach who had convinced me to come to ECU in the first place. First I was so angry with him, and then I just felt sad. I remember even crying about it at one point.

To make matters worse, I really did not connect with Coach Dye's replacement, Ed Emory. Coach Emory was a star guard during his playing days at ECU and well-respected in Greenville, but he was really different from Coach Dye. Here I was, on the verge of the senior season that was supposed to be the pinnacle of my college career, and I didn't believe in the leader of my team.

I made a decision that winter, after Coach Dye left. I made a practice of getting up at five in the morning and walking over to the basketball arena to run stairs indoors. Because I was going to be a senior, I decided that I needed to put my own feelings about the coaching change aside and become a strong team leader. My friend Mike Hawkins made the same resolution, and we really worked to create a smooth transition for the younger players, encouraging them and trying to lead by working harder than anyone else.

I was determined to make the most of that season, and that attitude prevailed even when I sustained a painful injury in preseason camp. My approach to that injury, and the help I got from team trainers, started a trend that would turn into a major issue in my life as my career unfolded.

During practice one day, I got hit in the ribs really hard, and I knew right away that it was something bad. My ribs were killing me the next day, but I wanted to suck it up, because I was a leader. I didn't tell anyone at first, but eventually I went to the team trainer and told him that I thought I might have bruised my ribs and I needed a flak jacket to cover them up during practice.

It turns out I didn't bruise my ribs—I cracked them. But in those days, if a player wanted to play through pain the trainers would do whatever they could to enable them. So a trainer started giving me shots of painkiller so that I could still function on the field—one at the beginning of the game, one at halftime and one when the game was over. When I didn't have the medicine I was in so much pain—I couldn't sleep, and forget about sneezing or coughing. So I would go back to the trainer for another shot when it got too bad, and the pain went away, but the medicine upset my stomach. It wouldn't be long before I would find a solution for the nausea that would lead me down a destructive path.

Ed Emory eventually brought the Pirates to a national ranking in 1983, but his first season, 1980, was a losing 4-7 campaign, a far cry from the winning tradition Coach Dye had established. The offense was struggling so much that I couldn't be very productive, and I finished my senior year with only 535 total yards, fewer than half of my total from my junior season. But I was still able to turn heads as a senior in another area—in the kickoff return game.

Ironically, the play I am best remembered for among Pirates fans came in our most lopsided defeat of the season.

It was our third game, at Florida State, and on the opening kickoff of the game I caught the ball and ran it back 105 yards for a touchdown. That return still stands in the ECU record books as the longest kickoff return in school history. I ran for a total of 207 kickoff return yards in that game, which is another school record, but unfortunately we got our tails kicked, losing 63-7.

More than three decades later, I was still sixth overall for average kickoff return yards in a season (26.8 in 1980) and fourth overall in average kickoff return yards over a career (24.5). And when NFL teams began to talk to me seriously, they wanted to talk about how I might contribute as a return specialist.

After stumbling in my academics as a freshman, I got it together and figured out what I needed to do to get by and stay eligible for football. Through the first semester of my senior year, I kept my GPA at about a 2.5 and went to class most of the time. But after football season ended and I took my exams for the fall semester, my focus turned completely toward preparing for the NFL. The way I saw it, I didn't need to worry about schoolwork anymore.

When football was over, I got this great idea that I was going to stop going to class and forget about school. I decided I should use that extra time to work out even harder, since my only goal was to impress the NFL scouts. I really didn't think about my education, because college graduation was not my goal. Neither one of my parents had finished high school, and they never pushed us much about college. If not for football, I probably would have stopped my education in high school and gone to work for my dad's construction company.

I was really taking a risk, and I know now that I was given a gift from East Carolina—free education—and I threw it away. I remember a standout player who was a year older than me at ECU—everyone thought he was going to be drafted. Just like me, he stopped going to class during that spring semester and put all of his eggs in the pro football basket. Then draft day came, he had all kinds of media at his house, and his name wasn't called. I felt really bad for him at the time, but that didn't get me out the door when it was time for class during my final semester.

Today I have the opportunity to speak to top high school athletes all over the country, and I am passionate about reminding them to finish their college education. I truly believe that if someone had harped on me about the importance of education I would have made it more of a priority. Whenever I talk to young football players, I encourage them to keep their big dreams alive but to add another goal—a college degree. I have known so many NFL players who made a lot of money for a few years, blew through that cash and suddenly their football careers were over without anything to fall back on.

Later in my life, at the age of fifty-two, I did graduate from East Carolina University, and finishing that degree was one of the hardest things I've ever done, because I had been out of school for so long. But that diploma is truly one of my most treasured possessions.

Another significant thing that happened when I was a senior is that I met my future wife, Sam. I fell in love with her, and during our senior year we moved in together and she kind of took care of me, especially through that rib injury. My parents went to see their family in Florida for Christmas that year, and Sam and I drove down for a visit. It was a disaster.

She did not get along well with my parents, and I started to wonder if she was the one for me. But back in North Carolina, our relationship was better, and she provided some stability through an uncertain time in my life.

In February of my senior year, I was invited to participate in the NFL Scouting Combine in Indianapolis, which is a showcase for the top collegiate players in the country. My roommate at the combine was Howie Long, who went on to a stellar Hall of Fame career as a defensive lineman with the Raiders and then became a studio analyst for Fox. I also got to know other future Pro Bowlers like Hanford Dixon and Kenny Easley, guys I would soon be playing against.

After the combine, I kept working out and waiting to hear from teams that might be interested. The Washington Redskins were the only squad that actually invited me up for a visit, and they told me that they were hoping to get me in the fifth or sixth round as a return specialist. I really didn't care which round I was selected in; they had twelve rounds back then, and I just wanted to be on some team's board.

When the school year was over, I won the award for the best overall athlete at East Carolina. I didn't know where my address would be that summer, but I knew I was on the move and that I was standing in the doorway of my dream. I had worked as hard as I possibly could, I had racked up the kind of stats that made me an attractive prospect for a pro team, and I had a girlfriend who loved me and looked after me. Suddenly the goal that had looked so distant when I was a little Pop Warner player in Penn Yan was within easy reach.

• • •

CHAPTER FOUR

ROOKIE YEAR

Dreams do come true.

As NFL Draft Day approached in the spring of 1981, I didn't have to think too hard about where I wanted to be when the names were called. I hadn't forgotten the embarrassing scenario my teammate faced a year earlier, when he gathered the media and a bunch of friends for the spectacle and found himself undrafted. I felt pretty good about my chances, but I wasn't about to put myself in a situation like that.

So that Saturday, it was just me and my girlfriend Sam, in our little apartment, sitting on the couch across from our twelve-inch TV. As we watched, two of my friends from the Indianapolis Combine were picked in the first round—Kenny Easley went fourth overall to Seattle and Hanford Dixon was picked 22nd by Cleveland. Other players who went on to pro stardom from that year's first round were Lawrence Taylor and Ronnie Lott.

There were twenty-eight total picks in the first round, and so after those big announcements Sam and I settled in to watch the second round with low expectations. After all, I had been told to pay extra close attention starting in the fifth round or so.

I heard other players selected, guys like Mike Singletary and Cris Collinsworth that would one day become household names. And two-thirds of the way through the second round, with the 47th pick overall, I got the happiest surprise of my life. I had been picked by the New England Patriots.

At that time, no East Carolina player had ever been selected higher than me in the NFL draft. Just as I was seeing my name on TV and trying to process it, my apartment phone rang, and it was an executive from the Patriots confirming that those words on the screen—Anthony Collins in the second round to New England—were true.

The Patriots coaching staff, led at that time by Ron Erhardt, told me that they were bringing me in to return kicks. But as much as I loved setting off fireworks in the return game, I was still holding fast to my desire to play running back in the pros. That day, in that little apartment, with my mom and my dad and my brothers and sisters calling to congratulate me, anything seemed possible. That big dream, the one that falls by the wayside for thousands of young football players every year, was finally in my hands.

Because I was one of the first two players selected, the Patriots flew me and first-round pick Brian Holloway up to Foxborough to meet the media. Even though I had grown up in the Northeast, I really had no idea where the New England Patriots were based when I received that first phone call, and even when I was on my way there I thought I was going to Boston. Well, Foxborough is in the Boston area, but it's a small town full of mostly white people. It actually reminded me a lot of Penn Yan.

When Brian and I arrived and they picked us up at the airport, I had quite a few surprises waiting. First of all, they were putting us up in the Red Fox Hotel, a hole in the wall right next to Sullivan Stadium. It was a far cry from the fancy metropolitan hotel I had imagined. Then we got a tour of the stadium, and it was much shabbier than the NFL facilities I had seen on television. The weight room was tiny—much smaller than our weight room at East Carolina. A year after that, they renovated and expanded everything, but in 1981 it was far from cutting-edge, and I remember feeling a little disappointed.

Still, I was an NFL player, and not even a pitiful weight room was going to take away my excitement that spring. I remember doing a bunch of media interviews—I had only ever talked to a handful of reporters down in Greenville—and I said the same thing over and over, "I'm just thankful to be here." I meant it. I really was thankful for the opportunity that was being given to me.

Right after that visit, the rookies had to report to our first minicamp, and the veterans came a couple of days later. After every workout, I was being requested for more media interviews, partly because the team executives were taking heat for selecting me in the second round and the reporters were trying to figure me out. I knew that I was getting a bad rap before I even played a down, and that made me want to prove myself even more. After everyone was done with the minicamp practices, I would run stadium steps and do more squats. I remember the other guys looking at me, saying, "You're crazy! What are you doing?"

Shortly after the draft, Sam and I went to my old teammate Eddie Hicks' wedding in Henderson, North Carolina I really had not planned on getting married at that point; I was thinking that Sam would come up to Massachusetts with me and we would just live together. But her mom had been talking to her, telling her that if I truly loved her I would marry her.

I guess Eddie's wedding festivities, along with Sam's persistence, must have given me the wedding bug, because suddenly I was sure that Sam and I should get married as soon as possible. One of the question marks in my life—my NFL future—had been answered definitively, so I guess I was seeking stability everywhere. I was pretty immature, but I thought I knew what it took to make a marriage work. And I believed that I truly loved Sam at the time, although I understand now that if I really loved her I wouldn't have been cheating on her.

Looking back, I think I admired my father so much that I wanted to emulate the happy, faithful, large family of my childhood. I had been given a great model of the value of family, and I knew that I wouldn't have made it to that Draft Day without my parents' steady influence. I wanted to take the first step in creating a home like that. The problem was, my father was a man of discipline and integrity driven by his unwavering faith in God. At that point in my life, I was just a guy with a pattern of womanizing who had accomplished one great thing.

I can see now that the prospect of a happy and stable union between Sam and me was on shaky ground from the start. But I was full of youthful optimism then, and I knew she could help take care of me in a new city. So just a few days before I left for training camp, with Sam wearing a ring I had purchased with part of my $60,000 signing bonus, we were married in a small ceremony in Greenville. Only a few of our friends were present; my family didn't approve of the marriage and didn't get along with my new wife, so I thought it best if they didn't come.

Sam and I moved into an apartment in Attleboro, Massachusetts to start our new life together. When my agent Ken Hutcherson negotiated that huge signing bonus—more money than I had ever seen in my whole life—I was pretty sure I was going to be happy as a Patriot.

There were some talented athletes ahead of me at the running back position in New England. The top returning back was Vagas Ferguson, a first-round pick out of Notre Dame the previous year who finished fifth in the Heisman voting in 1980. Most observers were sure that Ferguson had the starting job locked up, but Horace Ivory—a four-year NFL veteran—and a former Northern Arizona back named Allan Clark had the strength and speed to give him a fair fight for it.

Clark and I never actually played together—he tore his ACL in training camp and was out for the season—but he had already been a Patriot for two years when I arrived, and his seniority meant a new name for me. I had been Anthony Collins, or 'AC' my whole life, but in Foxborough they told me that they already had an 'AC' and I needed to start calling myself Tony Collins. I didn't like it at first, but I agreed, and I never went back to Anthony.

From my first workout as a Patriot, I quietly declared open season on the starting halfback slots. Of course, Ferguson seemed like a lock, and I was a rookie from a university many people had never heard of. If I wanted to be discouraged about my chances of lining up in the backfield, I just needed to pick up the Boston Globe, where Coach Erhardt told a sportswriter, "We'll be using Vagas in running situations, and he's our number one guy."

When the Patriots used their second-round pick on me, the team's brass took some criticism. According to the draft pundits, I had a reputation for avoiding the tackle by running to the sideline, so therefore I wasn't tough enough to hang in the NFL trenches. I knew that wasn't true, and even if training camp wasn't the place to prove myself in a full-tackle scenario, I could show off my skills enough to make the coaches glad they took a chance on me.

The Patriots held their training camp at tiny Bryant College in Smithfield, Rhode Island, and in late July—just a few days after we moved in—the media was declaring me a promising newcomer. Just before our first preseason game against the Rams, Vagas was still at the top of the depth chart, but my name was coming up as a possible candidate for passing situations.

We defeated the Rams 31-7 and Vagas did get most of the carries, but I made an impression too. According to the Boston Globe, "The drive for the Patriots' third touchdown may someday be remembered more for the debut of second-round draft choice Tony Collins, who carried nine times in the second quarter for 51 yards."

Ferguson and Ivory were both injured later in the preseason—not serious enough to be out for the year, but serious enough to put them both out of commission for the early season games. So, as one Patriots beat writer was declaring me the Most Spectacular Rookie in training camp, I got the starting nod at halfback, and I kept it for most of the season. Ivory was traded to Seattle in late September, and Ferguson became my backup.

I was exactly where I wanted to be, but unfortunately my team was struggling. We lost our first four regular-season games, despite the promise we seemed to show in the pre-season. Boston Globe writer Michael Madden wrote a feature story about me after the second of those losses, and the story declared me a bright spot in a frustrating early season:

> Lost amid the Patriots' two losses has been Tony Collins, a rookie who needed no time to find a place in pro football. In happier times, a rookie starting his career as Collins has done would be cause for joy. The second-round choice from East Carolina has picked up 81 and 71 yards in his first two games, caught six passes and has shown that he is extremely durable. A workhorse actually, as he carried the ball 15 times his first game and 18 times last Sunday against the Eagles. And the work has been necessary. With both Vagas Ferguson and Horace Ivory missing the first two games with injuries, coach Ron Erhardt's revolving door at halfback has been stuck on Collins in run situations. And the rookie has not weakened under the heavy load.

The article mentioned the heat the Patriots took when they selected me in April and quoted me as saying that my reputation for avoiding contact actually helped light a fire under me as a rookie, because it gave me something to prove.

"I knew that was just talk, but I had to come in here and establish myself," I told Madden. "Everybody said the guy runs out of bounds all the time; that made me try harder."

I also confessed in the story that I was struggling during my senior year because of that rib injury, and I was really just looking out for myself because of my differences with the new ECU coach. I had come in lacking the kind of momentum that defined my junior year at ECU, but with a strong performance in camp and the early season I had found my swagger. "I feel good," I said at the time. "I've got my confidence back and I'm rolling."

I told the reporter that I had proven myself in the absence of Ferguson and Ivory and I knew I would get reps when they returned. But to keep my starting job was an even better outcome than I had dared to hope for. With every carry and every touchdown, I became even more confident that I was meant to be in the NFL. When Ivory was traded, the Patriots already had another great back, Sam Cunningham, but he was used at fullback and allowed me to keep my slot in the offense.

I knew I was building the coaches' confidence in me with every productive outing, and as the season progressed I kept getting my share of carries. I was one of the most consistent producers on offense until my rookie season hit its only real bump in the road—at an away game against the Bills. Because Buffalo is only about two hours away from Penn Yan, my whole family and a lot of my friends from home were in the stands.

I didn't produce a very good homecoming show. I struggled in my running attack, gaining only five yards on four carries and fumbling the ball twice in that outing. After the second fumble, I was yanked from the game. I was incredibly disappointed in myself that day. I had been so excited to come home and play in front of everyone I loved, but things just went badly. It was snowing and cold, and I just couldn't hold onto the football. To make matters worse, the next day Coach Erhardt announced that he would be starting Vagas Ferguson the following week against St. Louis.

At that point I had collected 752 yards on 175 carries, and I was just 67 yards away from breaking the record for most rushing yards by a rookie that Ferguson himself had set the previous season. Even from the bench, I did end up owning that record—I finished the season with 873 total yards. I hated being benched—Coach Erhardt attributed my difficulties on the field to typical rookie fatigue, since an NFL season is so much longer than a collegiate season.

"It happens to most rookies in pro ball," he said. "They get beat up physically and mentally because they haven't gone through it before and don't know how to pace themselves."

At season's end, Boston Globe writer Will McDonough asked Erhardt for his assessment of his 1981 rookie class. He praised my field vision, instincts and quickness and said that I could have been a 1,000-yard runner that year if the coaching staff had pushed me more. He also said that one of my best assets to the team was my durability.

It might be true that I ran out of gas by November of that 1981 season, but for the most part I was blessedly healthy my rookie year. My ribs were healed, I was running full speed and I had managed to avoid any serious injuries. Soon enough I would become well acquainted with the team trainers, but I wasn't a regular visitor to the training room that year.

My personal life was pretty free of turbulence at that point as well. Sam and I were still newlyweds, we were still in love, and we were enjoying the new experience of having enough money to play and travel. We went to the Bahamas, Jamaica—places I had never even dreamed of as a kid in Penn Yan. But there were some storm clouds on the horizon—things I didn't want to acknowledge as problems.

I still liked women way too much, and I enjoyed the attention of the women who pursued me on the road. When I was at home, I was trying to be an attentive husband, but there was never a time in my marriage when I wasn't cheating on my wife on a pretty regular basis. And Sam still didn't get along with my family at all; here we were only a few hours from home, and I just started visiting New York alone to avoid the confrontations. She didn't respect my parents, and that was difficult for me to take. In retrospect, she kind of separated me from my family, and those blood relationships had always been my rock before.

Another area of regret that nagged me at that time was my nonexistent relationship with my daughter Nisi in New York, who had been born during my freshman year at ECU. I paid the child support, but I really wasn't involved in her life at all. Her mom got married and she eventually had a brother and sister, but I can't really say whether she had a happy childhood or not.

My wife wasn't happy about Nisi and didn't encourage me to connect with her at all, and I was so consumed with myself and my football career that I didn't push the point. Sam and I weren't very good for each other, even then when things looked OK, but I was still trying to do what the Bible says and leave and cleave, trying to build the kind of supportive and happy marriage that my parents had modeled. Looking back, I don't think I had a clue how to sacrifice myself out of love for another person.

I was fortunate that season—I was a rookie playing well at the position I coveted. So many players finally reach their dream only to crumble under the pressure of big-time competition, or they languish as a backup so long that they lose their intensity. But even if my ship was sailing along on stable waters personally, physically and athletically, I had entered an NFL that was defined by a culture of playing hard on the field and living life hard off of it.

Professional football in the eighties was populated by guys who played hurt and prided themselves in bone-jarring tackles.

Just two years before I came into the league, a legendary defensive end named Jack Youngblood had played in two playoff games and the Super Bowl with a broken fibula. The same players who gritted their teeth and bulldozed each other on the field also regularly pushed the envelope when it came to partying after the game. Drug testing was pretty much non-existent back then, and players weren't subject to the wall-to-wall media coverage that would emerge later. I was only wading at that point, but the rough waters were out there, and pretty soon I would be in over my head.

• • •

CHAPTER FIVE

PATRIOTS

Pride comes before the fall.

.

I entered the 1982 preseason with the world at my feet. I had enjoyed exceptional success as a rookie, my coaches considered me an asset and I was making more money than I had ever dreamed of. I had very few worries that summer, but trouble was brewing both for me personally and for the league that paid my salary.

The preseason and early season proceeded just as I had hoped. Our dismal 2-14 record in 1981 had spelled the end for Ron Erhardt, and we met our new coach, Ron Meyer, that January. Coach Meyer cleaned house in his first few months, cutting thirteen players from the existing roster, but even though both Vagas and I were still on the team I felt like the new coaching staff appreciated what I brought to the offense. In fact, during training camp he made it pretty clear that he wasn't looking to start a halfback controversy, telling a Boston Globe reporter, "Tony does everything a little better than Ferguson; he's a better runner, maybe has a little more speed, tremendous balance, better blocker, better receiver."

In our final exhibition game, a 41-27 rout of the Packers, I ran for 130 yards and caught two passes for 28 more. The offense that Meyer had brought to town seemed custom made for my abilities. Our season opener was more of the same—we defeated the Colts 24-13 and I led all rushers with 137 yards. Fans who had written us off after we landed in the toilet in the previous year were starting to believe in a resurgence directed by a young, energetic new coach and an offense that was racking up more yards than the Patriots had averaged in years. But on September 19, we looked more like our old selves with an anemic 31-7 loss to the Jets. As it turned out, the football public would have wait a while to find out which version of the Patriots was the real deal. The day after the Jets loss, just after a Monday night game between the Giants and the Packers, the season ground to a screeching halt.

The NFL Player's Association, directed by a lawyer named Ed Garvey, was holding the owners' feet to the fire by demanding that players receive fifty-five percent of the league's gross revenues. The owners refused, the union didn't budge, and suddenly the NFL season had been suspended indefinitely—the victim of a labor strike.

The strike went on for fifty-seven days, and during that time I kept myself busy by working out at a nearby gym three or four times a week and fervently hoping that the two parties would work out their differences. I remember thinking that the players who supported the NFLPA were crazy. I just wanted to play football.

It was extremely frustrating to be sitting at home during the heart of the season. The strike was divisive, even among players; many felt that we were justified in demanding the fifty-five percent, others thought that Garvey was causing too much drama and that the work stoppage was really just hurting everybody involved with the game. Finally, in mid-November, the negotiations moved past ego and petty concerns and became productive, and the result was a collective bargaining agreement satisfactory enough that practice could resume.

The agreement did calm the waters some, but the pro-union players in my locker room were far from appeased. The Patriots were known as one of the most union-friendly teams in the league, and the day after the agreement was announced we had a spirited players-only meeting that lasted more than an hour and started with sixteen of my teammates threatening to walk out on their own in a "wildcat strike." By the time the meeting had ended, our NFLPA representatives had convinced them to stay, but the tension was still evident around Patriot headquarters.

I wasn't one of the advocates of a wildcat strike, and more than anything I wanted to get back out there and continue what I had started in September. I even told the media that I hoped I could still reach 1,000 rushing yards in our shortened season, which resumed on November 21 and would include only nine games.

"Going back out again would be ridiculous," I told a reporter after that team meeting. "It wouldn't accomplish anything and it would probably end the whole season. It doesn't make any sense."

That season, which ended with a strange playoff creation called the Super Bowl Tournament, was certainly not the NFL at its best. After it was over, Detroit Lions owner William Clay Ford described it as "a Mickey Mouse playoff system and an asterisk season." My team finished 5-4, losing in the first round of the playoffs to the Dolphins. It wasn't overwhelming, but it represented a vast improvement over 1981.

The season might have been abbreviated, but in the time I was given to produce for the Patriots, I proved myself well. I finished the season as the Pats' leader in rushing yards, with 623, and second in receiving yards, with 187. And few people who watched me put up those numbers knew that a combination of addictive substances was helping me play through the pain I had suffered when I twisted my ankle early in the season.

Like I had with the rib injury at East Carolina, I went to see the team trainers, determined to keep running no matter what. And just like before, that training room door led to an easy and regular flow of painkillers that allowed me to keep my starting job. There's an old saying in football—"You can't make the club from the tub," and I had no intention of becoming another player with a bright start whose career was snuffed out by an injury.

Typically before a game, one of the trainers would give me a shot of painkiller that would dull the pain while I was on the field. Then after the game, my teammates and I regularly popped pills to avoid the soreness and aches that came from exerting so much effort on a Sunday. For me, there was only one problem with this cycle—the pain medicine upset my stomach, and that side effect was also threatening to harm my performance in the backfield.

I mentioned my stomach troubles to one of my friends on the team, and he gave me what seemed like an easy solution— smoke some marijuana to settle your stomach. Just two years earlier, I had distinguished myself from the guys in my college locker room as the one who rejected drugs in favor of donuts and milk, but I was in a different, more intense world now, and I readily accepted some pot from my friend.

Every time I took the painkillers I would also smoke some marijuana, but the guys I hung out with on the team smoked it even more regularly, and before long it became a daily thing for me. I would never get high before a game, but sometimes on the days when we had meetings and practice scheduled I would smoke a joint at nine in the morning. I would be high during the team meeting, eat lunch and then be fine by the time I took the field for practice.

We didn't worry about getting caught. Drug testing in the NFL was a joke back then. We were tested once at the beginning of the season, but that was all. Drug use was so commonplace that it was hard to find guys who weren't using some kind of illegal substance.

The marijuana made me feel more relaxed, and it fixed my indigestion from the pain pills and kept me in the best physical condition to keep playing at the top of my game. In retrospect, the pot was just a gateway to more hardcore drugs that would eventually spell the end of my football dream, but that year, as a twenty-three-year-old star, I felt invincible.

The other vice that put itself right in the middle of my path during my second season was the constant temptation presented by women. Wherever there are professional athletes on the road, there are women anxious for their company, and suddenly the womanizing tendencies that had been inside me for years took over. I didn't have the desire or the strength to say 'no,' and soon cheating on my wife became a weekly habit too.

It's unbelievable, in that era before cell phones and the Internet made communication simple, how easy it was to find women who were interested in no-strings-attached sex. One time during that second season, when we were playing in Atlanta, there was a knock on the door of my hotel. I pulled the door open and saw a beautiful woman wearing only a coat—which she opened up for me when I answered the door.

The womanizing only became more habitual as I entered my third season in the NFL, a season that was characterized by my best numbers as a pro. By that time, I had a woman in every pro city, and they knew how to find me within hours after I arrived in town. My teammates and I had girlfriends in New England, too, and they knew their way around the hotel where we stayed the nights before our home games. When it was time for lights out, we would hide women in the bathroom when the coaches came by for bed check, and then they would come out when the danger had passed. That was our routine, every home game.

A group of us also developed another routine, every Monday during the season. On Mondays we always had a short practice that ended about one, but none of us ever told our wives that we were getting finished that early. Instead of going home, we would go straight to this adult massage parlor place not too far from the stadium. We did that faithfully every Monday, like going to church.

There is no doubt in my mind, by this point in my marriage, that my wife knew what I was up to. We were more distant than ever, even though we were living under the same roof, and it seemed like most of the guys I knew viewed their marriages pretty casually too. I remember one time I got a note in my mailbox at the stadium, and it was from the wife of one of my teammates, asking me to meet her because she wanted to talk. It turned out she wanted to meet at a hotel and do more than talk, but I declined that particular meeting.

My wife would ask me questions about where I was or what I did when I was on the road, but I became skilled at lying to her. I didn't have the guts or the discipline to say 'no' to the constant temptation. I was playing good football, and I didn't see my flings as a distraction to my performance on the field.

Just like a parade of women became part of my pro football life, I continued to take pain pills whenever I thought an ache or a pain might slow me down in practice or a game. Football was still everything to me at that point, and I was determined not to miss practice for any reason, because I knew that if you didn't practice you didn't play. So if something was hurting, I just stopped by to see the team trainer and he would take care of it. I remember telling the trainer, "Give me whatever you've got to give me so I can get out on the field, because I don't want someone else to take my place." And of course, I kept smoking pot too, partly because it helped with the side effects from the painkillers and partly because I was hooked on the way it made me feel.

The irony of that 1983 season was that I was playing un-believable football. I was living those dream sequences I used to create in my bed, or in my backyard in Penn Yan. At some level, I must have known that I was developing habits that could one day destroy me, but it was tough to stop when the most important part of my life—football—was going so well.

My teammates and I were hoping that 1983 would be the year we would restore the Patriots' winning tradition that had put the team atop the AFC East five years earlier. We had a strong offensive line, and I was a major player on the offensive unit along with fan favorite Mosi Tatupu, a back from Hawaii who was one of my best friends on the team. (Mosi's death from unknown causes at age fifty-four was tough for me, because we played side by side. He was also mourned in Foxborough, where he played for thirteen seasons).

We lost our opener in overtime to a hapless Colts team, but I was putting up good numbers—averaging enough rushing yards to finally get that 1,000-yard season I had been hunting for.

I had plenty of highlights that season, like a 212-yard day against the Jets that was the top single-game rushing performance in Patriots history. (I'm still first in the team record books in that category). After that game, a Boston Globe story reported, "This game might be remembered as the one that made Tony Collins a big name in the NFL."

We were still up and down, with a 4-4 record at the midway point. With explosive outings like the Jets game and 94 yards in a big victory over the Chargers, I reached that 1,000-yard milestone—finishing the season with 1,049 yards and 10 touchdowns on the ground. The Patriots were 8-8 and second in the AFC East—decent, but not good enough.

It was a memorable season for me, and it was good enough for my greatest honor so far as an NFL player—selection to the Pro Bowl. I learned in December that I would be heading to Hawaii in January along with three of my teammates— punter Rich Camarillo and offensive linemen John Hannah and Brian Holloway. I remember that afternoon well—Coach Meyer gathered us together after practice and announced the names of the players who had been selected. It was really unexpected, because I didn't feel like my numbers were quite good enough to get me to the Pro Bowl, but it meant even more because my fellow players had voted for me.

As I prepared for my fourth season, a Pro Bowler with a rocky marriage and a budding drug addiction, I had figured out what I needed to do to put up stellar individual numbers. My next step as a football player was to become the kind of team leader that could carry the Patriots to new heights. I wanted to line up each Sunday for a team that was a legitimate Super Bowl threat.

Apparently Ron Meyer, who had succeeded in turning around the Southern Methodist team he coached before coming north to New England, was not the man to bring us there. Shortly after our eighth game of the 1984 season, a 44-24 home loss to Miami, Meyer was fired, and by the following Sunday we had a new head coach, Raymond Berry. We were 5-3 when Coach Meyer was canned, which was respectable, but our team executives wanted more than respectable.

I was once quoted as saying that Coach Berry earned more respect in our locker room in one day than Coach Meyer did in three years, and I meant it. Coach Meyer was not a bad guy, but he really didn't know how to motivate the older players. Coach Berry was a man of tremendous character, true Christian devotion and strong leadership, and we all noticed a difference with him at the helm. Before I had wanted to play well for myself, but Coach Berry made us want to succeed for him.

We didn't win every game after the midseason coaching change, but we did finish 9-7 and second in our division for our first winning record in five years. We had missed the playoffs again, but the mood in Foxborough was as optimistic as it had been since I had arrived, and Coach Berry would spend the offseason tweaking our roster to make us a team to be reckoned with.

The coaching change was definitely a positive thing for me, but my fourth year stands out for another, more personal reason—something that was more of a pitfall than a milestone. During the 1984 season I was introduced to cocaine by a Patriots teammate.

Suddenly, after years of telling myself that I was only taking pain pills and smoking marijuana because they aided my football career, I was taking a drug so addictive and altering that it could only hurt me as an athlete. When I first started with coke, I was snorting it, and I would only do it from time to time. I liked the high, but I really didn't like the way I felt when I came down. I had such a bad feeling after I used cocaine that I felt it would show on the field.

I wasn't the type of player who was known as a wild partier; despite my womanizing and the drug habit that was starting to grip me, a sportswriter in 1983 described me as "quiet and deeply religious." Early on, I was careful about how much cocaine I used during the football season, but it became a major distraction during the offseason. It hurt me. It hurt me a lot. With the cocaine, I didn't work out as much as I should have during the offseason. It was a big distraction.

I should have been using that time to lift weights and run, or maybe to spend time with my family—I learned that my wife was pregnant with our first child during that 1984 season. But pretty soon the allure of cocaine pushed everything else out of the picture. Around that time, my wife started using cocaine too, and that made me even more tempted. We were not good for each other at all.

The sports world was aware of cocaine's prevalence in the NFL, thanks to a groundbreaking 1982 article in Sports Illustrated. In the article, former NFL defensive end Don Reese detailed his downward spiral into cocaine addiction and the drug-fueled detonation of his seven-year pro career. In some ways, Reese was telling my story, only he left the league just as I was coming in. He actually had to spend a year in jail for selling cocaine, but after he was released from jail he was picked up by the New Orleans Saints, where he got involved with freebasing and his addiction only intensified. According to Reese, teams like the Saints were so dominated by the drug culture that it affected the win-loss record, the locker room environment and everything about the squad.

"If you care about the game you have to be alarmed," Reese said in the article. "What you see on the tube on Sunday afternoon is often a lie. When players are messed up, the game is messed up. The outcome of games is dishonest when playing ability is impaired."

Unlike teams like the Saints, the Patriots weren't known as a big drug team during those years, but I knew quite a few players on my team and others who were using. Before long my addiction became even more dangerous when I was introduced to a new method of ingesting the drug—the technique that we called freebasing.

Freebase cocaine was a purified form of the powder, and to make it users like me had to cook it down using a dangerous process involving fire and ether or baking soda. In 1980, comedian Richard Pryor drew attention to the practice when he set himself on fire while freebasing cocaine and suffered burns over more than half of his body. During the time I started using, freebasing was becoming more and popular among drug users who could afford the drugs and the materials—Hollywood types and professional athletes.

My daughter Colette was born in May of 1985. I was in the delivery room when she was born, and I was so excited and so happy that day. I had not had the chance to see my first daughter grow up, and I couldn't wait to take care of Colette and be part of her life. I even said to myself, "This is a new start. I'm going to stop messing around with women and be faithful to my wife." That resolution lasted about a month.

With minimal football responsibilities that spring, I was free to chase drugs and women, and there is no doubt that I paid for it when I returned to training camp in July. But at that point I was a big-time veteran, with a 1,000-yard season under my belt, and I felt pretty much untouchable. What started as an innocent boy's big dream had soured, deteriorating into a lifestyle that supported and enabled the destruction of my family and my body. Don Reese, speaking to Sports Illustrated, had strong feelings about the NFL and its role in exposing him to illegal drugs.

"Football—the environment, not the game itself—as good as wrecked my life," said Reese, who died in 2003 from liver cancer. "I should have been smarter. I should have been stronger. I know that. But drugs dominate the game, and I got caught up in them, and before I knew it I was freebasing cocaine. And then I was a zombie."

The NFL was certainly not responsible for my drug problem, but in those years there was plenty of denial and very little accountability about the issue. I had lots of free time during the offseason, teammates who knew how to get the drugs and were more than willing to party with me and enough money to buy as much cocaine as I wanted. It would take countless bad decisions before I would finally face the only consequence that would truly sting.

• • •

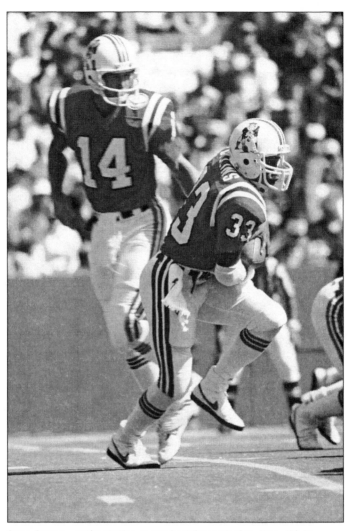

Steve Grogan was the starting quarterback for most of my time with New England, and we worked well together. Grogan is third in all-time passing yards behind Tom Brady and Drew Bledsoe.

Here I am eluding tacklers from the backfield against the New York Jets. I am still the third all-time leading rusher in Patriots history, with 4,647 total yards.

I loved seeing that stretch of open field in front of me.

I was one stylish teenager growing up in Penn Yan. Look at that hat!

Penn Yan Academy was a small school, but our football program was respected throughout New York. That's me with my teammate and best friend Tom Watkins.

Becoming a grandfather has been one of the great joys of my life. Here my grandson Jayden tries on a Patriots hat.

In 2009 we had a photo shoot for the whole Collins family, including the dog. I'm right in the center, and the back row, from left, are Conredge, TJ, Colette, Terrie and my grandson Antonio. In the middle row are Nisi and her baby son Tyson, Toni, Taylor and Alisha. In the front row are my grandson Baylor, Trudy and our dog Gunther and my granddaughter Angi.

Bob Brudzinski was one of the Dolphins' toughest linebackers, but I rolled past him on this run on a wet day in Foxborough.

The best games were the ones where my pants had so much dirt on them that you could hardly see the white.

This photo, and the statements above it, really sum up my journey. I am grateful for the chance to touch others' lives through my struggles.

ECU School of Communication
Graduate Recognition Ceremony
May 6, 2011

My graduation from East Carolina University in 2011 was a proud day for me. Here I receive my diploma from Dr. Linda Kean, the director of the school of communication.

When I walked across that stage to receive my diploma, many of my family members were there celebrating with me, which made the accomplishment even more special.

My return to Greenville, North Carolina, the place that greeted me as a young player with big NFL dreams decades ago, has provided the ideal setting for my new life.

Several years ago Trudy and I went to the Patriots new home, Gillette Stadium, for an annual event called "The Game With the Greats." Here we pose in front of a photo of me in my New England glory days.

I struggled with the idea of commitment in marriage for many years, but when I met Trudy I finally understood what it means to truly share life with someone.

Through countless ups and downs, Trudy has always been my number one encourager.

CHAPTER SIX

THE FALL

To be successful, you must surround yourself with good people.

The 1985 season will always stand out for me because it contained one of the highest highs of my career—reaching the Super Bowl, just weeks before the lowest low so far—a public spotlight on my drug problem. In fact, I doubt that the embarrassment over my drug abuse coming out in the papers would have even happened if my team hadn't finally reached the pinnacle of professional football.

My offseason was muddied by escalating cocaine use and the careless womanizing that had become routine for me. I had become a father for the first time that May when my daughter Colette was born, but I was too wrapped up in my bad habits to care for my baby the way a daddy should. When the preseason rolled around, though, I tried to regain my focus for the one thing that could still divert my attention from getting high—succeeding on the football field.

Craig James had signed with the Patriots the previous year and was playing well at halfback, so for much of that season I was still starting in the backfield but I was spending most of my time blocking for Craig. He finished the season with an impressive 1,227 yards on the ground, and I got some of the credit for his productivity. But I wasn't completely behind the scenes—I had 657 yards on the ground and 549 in the air that year for my most balanced offensive contribution so far.

Our coach, Raymond Berry, took some criticism for shuffling the personnel in the backfield, benching me for a short time in the middle of the season and moving James to fullback at one point. But eventually he figured out that his best tactic was to hand the ball to James, and one result was that my Patriots got in the habit of winning. We finished the regular season 11-5, which was our best record in years, but certainly not the best in the league. We only made the playoffs as a wild card team because of a tiebreaker system, and we were considered a long shot to advance past the first round.

In the playoffs, we beat the Jets and the Raiders and then rolled over the Dolphins 31-14 in the conference championship, defeating Miami for the first time in sixteen years. That Miami victory was one of my most memorable as a pro. My wife and my baby daughter came down there, and I played really well that day. It was a great victory for me.

The New England Patriots, with little Tony Collins from Penn Yan playing a vital role, were heading to the Super Bowl for the first time in history. We would face a talented Chicago team that had only lost once—to Miami. So even though the Bears were strong, we felt like we had what it took to give them a run for their money.

Of course, my teammates and I might have been winning, but we weren't slowing down on the partying one bit. In fact, the parties got wilder when we had more victories to celebrate. During that season, I bought a souped-up van—basically a partymobile—and my friends on the team liked to pile in the van with me to look for a good time.

After the first-round playoff win over the Jets, a bunch of guys jumped in my van and we stayed out all night long. We were doing some hardcore celebrating, but we knew we had to be back at Sullivan Stadium the next morning at about nine for meetings and a workout. I'll never forget what greeted us when we pulled back into the parking lot that morning—all of our wives, waiting for us with grim looks on their faces.

We didn't realize it at the time, but one of the girls with us at one of those parties that night was an assistant to a Boston Globe reporter. She certainly saw plenty of newsworthy things, but nothing came out at the time. Our angry wives were enough to deal with. Soon we forgot about it and turned our attention to the Raiders.

Fast forward a month, to Super Bowl XX in New Orleans. Every Super Bowl is a big spectacle, but because this was the twentieth championship it attracted even more attention than normal. All of the former MVPs from the first nineteen Super Bowls came back to be honored at halftime, and both the Patriots and the Chicago Bears were making our first-ever Super Bowl appearance.

Unlike us, the Bears had dominated during the regular season, finishing 15-1 behind colorful players like quarterback Jim McMahon and lineman William "Refrigerator" Perry. They had outscored their opponents 456-198 that year, so we certainly had our work cut out for us.

Given the two teams' recent histories, it came as no surprise to the nation's football fans when the Bears trounced us 46-10 in one of the most lopsided Super Bowl losses in history. To this day, it hurts me to repeat this statistic: the dominating Chicago defense set a new Super Bowl record for fewest rushing yards allowed, only giving our backfield seven yards in the entire game. We scored first, early in the first quarter, and it was all downhill from there.

We were overmatched, and the Cinderella factor wasn't enough to carry us past that dominant Bears squad. But in the days after the loss, instead of focusing solely on the statistics or the many strengths that Chicago brought to the Superdome, the media found something else to put a spotlight on—drug use among the Patriot players.

The morning after the loss, Coach Berry called a team meeting in New Orleans and dropped a bombshell—he told us that a Boston Globe reporter had been investigating drug abuse on our team and had names and dates. We learned that his series on the drug problem could run anytime. (The first story in the series by the reporter, Ron Borges, ran the next day). Berry also proposed a one-year mandatory drug testing program for the team and urged us to vote in favor of it. He hinted that if we didn't agree to his plan to clean up our locker room, he would resign.

We voted for the drug testing plan, and the Boston Globe stories started to spill details about the culture we had created for Patriots who were willing to party—freebasing, free sex, all-night parties with little regard for our coaches or our families. Borges' first story didn't name names, but the second one did —listing the names of six Patriots who had used drugs and stating that the identity of those players had been confirmed by our coaching staff. One of the names was Tony Collins.

I met with Coach Berry and agreed to drug counseling and regular testing. He was known as one of the most straight-laced coaches in the NFL, and he was still considered a star from his playing days with the Colts. These drug revelations, and the heat he took personally following them, were the toughest challenges he had ever faced. After he asked us to vote on a team drug-testing program, he was criticized by the NFLPA for violating the collective bargaining drug agreement that came out after the 1982 Don Reese allegations, and many of the players were furious with him for letting their names be released to the media.

That episode didn't do anything to diminish my respect for Coach Berry, and I wasn't angry with him for his role in the drug revelations. My thought at that time was, "This is a wake-up call. I'm going to stop getting high and chasing women, because I love football more than I love those things." But my actions weren't consistent with that pledge. I was still hanging out with questionable women, and even when I stayed away from drugs for a while I continued womanizing. The girls would eventually lead right back to the drugs. I deluded myself into thinking that since I got caught once, nothing damaging was going to happen to my career again. But that newspaper series was actually the beginning of the end.

Like the Sports Illustrated article four years earlier, this was a loud wake-up call for NFL executives in denial about the level of drug abuse in their league. Just days after the Boston Globe stories broke and other media across the country had jumped on the story, NFL commissioner Pete Rozelle told one group of reporters that he wished everyone would just focus on the Bears and the Super Bowl TV ratings. Sports Illustrated, in a critical story on February 10, wondered if the players themselves were going to have to clean up their sport, noting that the owners, coaches and union representatives seemed unwilling to take definitive action.

"In the end the long-suffering Patriots finally reached the Super Bowl, only to lose the game and be further embarrassed by the drug revelations," the story said. "A parade in the Pats' honor had been scheduled for this week but the club canceled it, insisting, unconvincingly, that the drug situation had nothing to do with it."

When the waters from that controversy finally settled, we were embarrassed by the attention, but that was about it. We knew that we should expect some drug testing, but we were still getting high regularly and searching for ways to keep the stuff from being detected. We tried the craziest methods—I remember one time we drank vinegar to clean out our systems. And the team trainers were our friends, so they would tell us when our name was coming up for the testing, which would motivate us to stay clean for a few days.

I had actually already failed a drug test, at the beginning of the 1985 season, but I only got a slap on the wrist and I had become more skilled at manipulating the system. In the 1986 offseason, I tested positive for cocaine again, and that time Coach Berry made me go to rehab. I agreed, because it was what I had to do to stay on the team.

I went down to Houston and checked into a drug rehab center, but I didn't take it seriously. To me, rehab was a joke, and I didn't really want to get better, so the process didn't mean anything to me. The whole thing was supposed to be hush-hush—I went by the name Larry while I was there—but about two weeks after I arrived the truth came out in the papers, prompting a tearful phone call from my wife and fueling my reputation as a Patriot with a drug problem.

I pretty much faked my way through rehab, but there was one part of it that I really hated. At the beginning of every meeting, I had to say, "My name is Larry and I'm a drug addict." I hated that, because I really didn't feel like an addict. I still wanted to use drugs, and I still thought I could manage my life even while I was getting high. But I have always believed that words have power, so it hurt me to say that in front of people every day.

After thirty days in Houston, I went back to Foxborough and faced Coach Berry, who was kind to me even when I didn't deserve it. He never hollered or screamed, and he was always such a fair coach. I believe he was genuinely trying to help me, and I really wish I hadn't put him through so much.

For a while, after I checked out of rehab, I tried to stay clean. It didn't take long for me to start smoking pot again, but I stayed away from cocaine. I still had the inside scoop from the trainers on the drug testing schedule, so I was sure I could avoid being busted again. Still, even when I was avoiding drugs I was on the lookout for women. I loved my kids, but I was so unhappy in my marriage that I didn't have much incentive to behave.

My only refuge was football. It was like the football field was my kingdom, and I could be at peace there. When I didn't have any football to play, I was just unsettled. But my dominion in that kingdom was drawing to an end. I had failed two drug tests with the Patriots, and Coach Berry was keeping me on an extremely short rope.

The 1986 season was a chance for a fresh football start after the controversy that had capped off our Super Bowl run. That summer, our squad was overcrowded at the running back position, and rumors that I would be traded even cropped up in the papers. But our front office quickly put those to rest, and we set out to prove that we could build on our 1985 postseason run.

Unfortunately, we had lost a couple of our top offensive lineman from that team, and our running game seemed stagnant during the first half of the season; after four games Craig James was averaging only 3.1 yards per carry and I was only gaining 2.7. But I was catching the ball more than ever, and despite our tension that winter Coach Berry told a reporter that I was "the best all-around back in football."

That season marked the only time that I collected more yards in the air (684) than on the ground (412), and my 77 receptions set a new Patriots record for most catches in a season by a running back. We were 3-3 early, plagued by our sluggish offense, but then we went on a seven-game winning streak and finished the season 11-5 again and in first place in the AFC East. Our hopes of a second Super Bowl trip, though, were dashed with a first-round playoff loss to the Broncos.

Personally, my sixth NFL season was more of the same—drugs and women filled much of my free time and my family was pushed to the sideline, despite the birth of my son Conredge in October of 1986. I successfully tap danced around the team's drug testing routine, and as far as Coach Berry knew the rehab had worked and I had shut the door on the drug culture. The reality, of course, was that as rehab receded into my memory I sank deeper into freebasing cocaine and living from high to high.

The final straw with the Patriots, the team that had handed me my NFL dream on that shiny second-round platter six years earlier, came during the 1987 season. I was still contributing that year—I had 474 rushing yards and 347 receiving yards—but after the season I learned that my name was coming up for a random drug test the following day. I knew I wasn't clean, and no amount of vinegar was going to bail me out.

I refused the test, thinking that a question mark was better than a third positive. Of course, declining to be tested was considered the same thing as failing the test, and the NFL drug policy was clear—three strikes and you're suspended. But Coach Berry made a different choice, because he was a good man and I had meant so much to the Patriots. Rather than give me the suspension I deserved, he quietly released me during the offseason, and I said goodbye to Foxborough for good.

My old New England coach Ron Meyer had taken over as head coach of the Indianapolis Colts, and when he heard that I was available he asked me to report to the Colts as a free agent. I was thrilled to get another chance to play—the Colts were an up-and-coming team and I would share the backfield with the great Eric Dickerson.

Coach Meyer made it clear from the beginning that I would not be free to do whatever I pleased in Indianapolis and that I could only suit up if I stayed completely drug-free. I agreed to every condition he placed on me, including daily testing and support meetings several times a week. With my release from the Patriots I had a glimpse of a harsh reality— that my drug habit could erase my football career. That sobered me up pretty quick, and in my early weeks in Indy I passed every drug test and dutifully went to the meetings, getting pretty good at saying, "Hi, my name is Tony Collins and I'm a drug addict."

I knew I would be crazy to smoke weed or cocaine, and I stayed away from the stuff. But I made one stupid mistake that summer that altered the course of my life. During the third week of that preseason, I went to a party with some teammates, and there were plenty of drugs there. It wasn't like a regular party. It was more like an orgy.

I stayed at that party for hours, but I didn't touch marijuana or cocaine. Still, apparently I was around enough of the smoke for it to get into my system somehow. The next day at the Colts headquarters, I took my drug test like always with a clean conscience.

Two days later, Coach Meyer called me into his office. I honestly thought I was heading in there for a friendly chat about how well I had been playing in training camp. Instead, he dropped the bombshell that I had failed a drug test. I told him, "No, I didn't use anything," but who was really going to believe me?

That was a dark day for me. It was actually my fourth strike, and my third official positive test. Myers told me that the NFL was suspending me for one year.

All of a sudden, my well-constructed house of cards was in a pile at my feet. I had carried on for years producing good numbers at the highest level of football while still using cocaine and marijuana on a regular basis. I should have known that it was only a matter of time before my bad choices caught up with me and I lost the thing I valued most. But when the league took football away from me, I was in complete shock.

The news could not have come at a worse time. Just a few days earlier, I had bought a house in Indianapolis, and my wife and kids were scheduled to come out any time. In fact, they moved to town the day the official announcement of my suspension was made. It was a nightmare.

We lost the down payment on our house and moved into a little town house. Playing football was the only job I had ever strived for, the only thing I had ever worked toward and the part of my life that made me feel alive. Suddenly, with one wild party, I was facing my first fall in fifteen years without football.

And the worst part of the whole sad episode was that I had actually been keeping myself clean.

I believe strongly that everything happens for a reason, and even though I had plenty of rough road ahead I think that God let my suspension happen so that I would eventually change my life and devote myself to helping other people. Of course, none of that occurred to me at the time. I was just angry and frustrated at the circumstances, and even more so because nobody believed my version of the story. My wife and my agent both said that they believed me, but they really thought I had been using.

Here I was, in an unfamiliar city, where fans didn't even know me yet and my friends and family were hundreds of miles away. My Colts teammates were playing preseason games, holding press conferences and preparing for their season opener against the Houston Oilers. I had no paycheck, no prospect for making money, a damaged marriage and a drug addiction that I had never really faced head-on. Just two years earlier, I had been competing in the Super Bowl in one of the high points of my life. This, without a doubt, was the deepest valley.

■ ■ ■

CHAPTER SEVEN
THE BOTTOM

*God does not allow us to go through
anything we can't handle.*

Suddenly, in my mind, I was the victim. I had tried to make a
new start in Indianapolis—I was going to be clean, be a faithful
husband and be the hardest worker on the Colts practice field—
but I had failed a drug test I should have passed and now I was
done. Technically, of course, it was only a one-year suspension,
but it felt like the end of the world to me.

Since that grand plan had been destroyed, I went back to
my old coping methods—drugs and women. If the NFL was
going to punish me for getting high and I hadn't even been
using, then I was going to prove them right and get high as
much as I wanted. That was the kind of logic that was driving
my actions in those days.

I had been introduced to freebasing earlier, but when I was
suspended I got really serious about smoking cocaine instead
of snorting it. Freebasing, or smoking crack, gives you a much
more intense high and as a result it is even more addictive than
snorting. It's also more expensive. When I was snorting the
powdered cocaine, I might spend $50 to $100 on each buy, but
when I switched to crack I would spend $800 or $900 each time,

because it took so much more of the drug to cook it down to the freebase form.

I had saved some money from my NFL salary, but in just a matter of weeks the daily need for drugs was ruling both my wife and me. And when an addict needs drugs, the price or the wisdom of depleting a savings account aren't important. The money to buy the drugs was there, so we spent it until it was gone. It didn't take very long.

One particular snapshot from that chapter in my life breaks my heart. Sam and I were living in that townhouse, and our main pastime was smoking crack. But we had these two little kids at the time—Colette and Conredge were three and one—and they desperately wanted and needed our attention. I remember the kids crying, wanting us to respond, and we couldn't do much of anything for them because we were too busy getting high. On a typical day, we would take them to the day care center down the street, go home and start freebasing cocaine.

At that point, drug use was the only thing keeping Sam and I together, and she didn't even have the income or the glory of being an NFL wife anymore. So that December, about three months after my suspension, my wife and kids left Indianapolis and drove back to her hometown of Creedmoor, North Carolina. When they left, I truly was alone. My parents and my brothers and sisters kept trying to call, but I avoided them and sank deeper into the Indy drug culture. Most addicts break ties with the people who love them, because their next high or their next drink becomes more important than friends or family. I was a classic example of that.

When I was playing football, I would mostly get high with teammates, in their nice houses or in the backrooms at clubs. In Indianapolis, I started frequenting seedy places like crackhouses. I could still find women for companionship, but the quality of women I was meeting now was much different than the NFL groupies who used to knock on my hotel doors. These were rough, desperate women—drug addicts like me.

I was trapped by my own bad choices, even though my predominant emotions during those months were anger and self-pity. I was angry at Coach Myers, angry with the NFL, angry with everybody who had a hand in stealing my NFL dream. I really didn't care what I did to myself or how badly I was hurting my loved ones. I felt like I was a failure, like everybody was ashamed of me and I had let everybody down.

My mom called me regularly, even though I'm sure it broke her heart every time. I had a car phone, and it seemed like she would always call when I was doing something I wasn't supposed to be doing. Inevitably, if I was on my way to buy drugs, or heading to a wild party or driving around with questionable women, that phone would ring and it would be Mom. Her calls were like reminders from God, that like my mom He still cared about me and He hadn't given up on me.

When I was growing up and even during my playing years, I always had this big smile and I was easy to get along with. Everybody loved Tony. Not only that, but since my first Pop Warner game, I had been told that I was a good football player. And because people affirmed me over and over as an athlete, I truly believed not only that I could thrive in the NFL, but that I could excel enough to make any team a winner. I had the confidence of someone who believes they can never lose, and the events of that fall proved me wrong in a big way.

I wouldn't wish that time in my life on my worst enemy, but I was going through it, and I had no motivation to better myself or find anything else that could give my life purpose. Football had been that thing, and it was gone.

It was that December, shortly after Sam and the kids left, when I had that close call with the cops and my car full of drug paraphernalia. Then came my lowest point yet—the overdose that resulted in the convulsions on the sidewalk and the mysterious man in black. I sent my brother and cousin away after their attempt at an intervention and made one bad choice after another. Later, they told me how difficult it was to return home to New York without me, especially when they had to face my mom and tell her that I was still deep into drugs. I can't imagine the strain and stress I put on my family.

Now it was early 1989, the season that had gone on without me was coming to an end, and I was trying to become a drug dealer. I don't know how an addict can really make any money as a drug dealer—the temptation to use the stuff before I sold it was too great. In the midst of that failed attempt, I had the other traffic stop on the way to Chicago and finally, early in the summer, the terrifying drive with my young son in North Carolina. When I left that car dealership, I had been spared either prison or death four separate times.

That episode in the car with Conredge was really an awakening for me. Getting suspended from the NFL hadn't reformed me one bit; in fact, it made me more dependent on drugs and women than ever. But I had almost killed my son. Over and over, I replayed that day and imagined how devastated I would have been if the crash had been worse, if I had survived and Conredge had died. But I believe that God did not allow that to happen. I have always told Conredge that he is here for a reason—that God spared him that day—and I started to believe the same thing about myself. When I was growing up I heard over and over that God loved me, but that summer I believed it—not only because I had survived, but because He hadn't let me go through the loss of my son.

Finally, I saw how pointless my life had become, saw what I was doing to my kids when they were counting on me. When I arrived in North Carolina, I was still focused on getting high, but suddenly I had a new purpose—to get my kids out of my wife's house. She had a boyfriend there and I didn't like that, and they were drinking and getting high all the time. My parents had moved to Florida to be closer to their family, and I decided that what we really needed was a fresh start in the Sunshine State.

I had some severance pay from the NFL—$104,000—and when I considered that money I finally made a good decision as a father. I put $25,000 away for each of my kids, and I had $54,000 left for myself. I told my wife that she was not in good shape to take care of the kids and I was taking them to Florida. My daughter was four and my son was two at the time, and when I first confronted my wife she was angry and said that she wasn't going to let them go. So I told her that I would give her all of that money, my share of the severance check, in exchange for my kids. She agreed, and we took off driving south.

We arrived in Sanford, Florida in time for the kids to start preschool that fall, and we moved in with my parents. For the first time in years I was close enough to my mom and dad to benefit from their good influence. My mom and dad had always been faithful Christians, and they were still going to church every week and serving the Lord in other ways. I decided that if I was really going to try to stay clean and provide stability for my kids, I needed a couple of things—a job and a church home of my own.

I found a great church called New Life Christian Center, and I immediately related to Pastor Ronald Murphy, who had been a college football player and had also been rescued out of drug addiction. He was really easy for me to talk to, and church offered the first genuine friendships I had experienced in a while. I went to worship services and Bible studies and made sure my kids learned the Biblical ideals that had guided my childhood.

I also got a job at Taco Bell, which is certainly a long way from the National Football League. But working at a fast food restaurant didn't really bother me at that point—I guess I had fallen too far to be proud and I had learned what happened when I had too much free time on my hands.

When I look back over the years when my life was on a downward slide, I realize what a grip the womanizing had on me. My cocaine and marijuana use was a huge problem, but at various times—when I would fail an NFL drug test, when one of my children was born—I would avoid getting high for weeks or months at a time. My drug abuse came in cycles, but until I moved to Florida I never really stopped seeking out women for flings.

In Sanford, working at Taco Bell and becoming a regular at church, I tried to put that addiction to rest. I wanted to stop sleeping around, but I had become so accustomed to the company of women that I was looking to fill that void. When I met a beautiful college basketball player named Sherod at church, I guess I fell in love with her, and I decided to try to add a stable relationship to the other changes I had made in my life.

I was thirty years old that fall, and Sherod was only nineteen. But not only was she beautiful and athletic, she was a good girl who was raised in the church. We started spending a lot of time together, and we got serious pretty quickly.

I told myself that our relationship was a positive thing, especially because I wanted a stable mother figure for my daughter Colette. Several months after Sherod and I started dating, she told me she was pregnant. I loved her and I wanted to do the right thing, so I asked her to marry me.

There was just one problem with my marriage proposal. I wasn't divorced from my first wife. We had been separated for close to a year (and the marriage was over long before that) but I just never felt the need to do anything about it legally, and Sam didn't push me. When Sherod asked me if I was legally divorced, I lied and told her I was. That's certainly not the foundation of trust you want to build a marriage on.

In the spring of 1990, Sherod and I went to the courthouse and got married. It was a marriage built on a lie, but in a way I think I held on to Sherod because she was a symbol of my new life, my effort to make good choices and do the right thing. For eight months, things were more stable than they had been in years.

I continued to go to church every Sunday, and I even became one of the leaders for a recovery program that helped drug addicts and alcoholics. I was living clean and told myself that I would never use drugs again, but the truth is I was still tempted by the allure of getting high. I tried to keep myself surrounded by positive people, and for a period I truly looked like a recovered, repentant addict.

My suspension had been lifted in the fall of 1989, and starting at that time an NFL representative would come from Tampa once a week to drug test me. I was tested regularly all the way through that season, and I was always clean. In June, I went up to New York to see NFL commissioner Pete Rozelle, and he reinstated me.

Finally, I was clear to play professional football again, but I had changed. The suspension and the nightmarish months that followed it had damaged my confidence, and even though I had tried to stay in shape I wasn't sure I could cut it back in the NFL. After my reinstatement, I stepped up my workouts, pushing myself as hard as I could.

That spring after the draft, I got two invitations for tryouts —from Miami and Detroit. Miami really liked me and brought me into training camp, and I did well enough to make the team. I signed a one-year contract for $100,000 and moved down to Miami to start what I hoped would be the next promising chapter of my football career.

The best part of my life as a Dolphin was our season opener, which was on the road against New England. I got to see my old teammates, and most of my family made the trip from New York. I only played on special teams, but we won the game and it was a good day.

The worst part of my Miami career? That Patriots game was my only outing as a Dolphin. Their top running back, Troy Stradford, was recovering from an injury and was returning to the roster, and they had too many backs. Coach Don Shula called me into his office a few days after the season opener and gave me the bad news—it was a numbers game, and they were going to have to release me. He told me to stay in shape and stay close, in case something changed.

That one game as a Dolphin marked my final play on an NFL field. I didn't want to admit it, but in training camp that summer I realized I had lost a step or two. My knees were really hurting—a result of running endless stadium steps and doing so many squats in my younger years and playing on turf in New England.

And I wasn't just struggling physically. After I got released Sherod and I were still living in a house in Miami, but we didn't have any income. My cousin Ed, who lived down there, came by to see me, and I remember him trying to encourage me because I was really down. It was like someone had resurrected my NFL dream, just enough to give me a ray of hope, and then the dream went dark again almost as quickly. I felt like I would have been better off if I had never tried to make a comeback at all.

My wife was pregnant—the baby was due in January of 1991—so we decided that our best course was to return to Sanford, back to family, friends and stability. We got settled in there again late that year, and soon after we moved my NFL hopes had one last revival when the Dolphins called at the end of the regular season.

Troy Stradford had suffered another injury, and they needed me to suit up for their first-round playoff game against the Colts. It was pretty amazing how my two Miami games were against my two former teams. The Dolphins paid me $10,000 to be available that day, in case anybody else got injured, but I never even got in the game. Miami won the game, and I went to a couple of practices before the next playoff game against Kansas City, but I didn't play that weekend, and in truth I was never really back on the squad.

After that quick re-entry into pro football, I returned to Sanford again, and soon I was a father for the fourth time when Alicia was born in January. This time, I wanted to do fatherhood differently. I was still reading the Bible, going to church and trying to do the right thing. I was still staying away from drugs and women and playing the part of the family man. I kept that up for a month or two, until a new football league came calling in February.

Like I've said, I know that through the rollercoaster years of my drug habit and my repeated affairs I was in control of my own choices. I might have behaved like a victim at times, but I am aware that I could have avoided all of the temptations if I had been stronger. But something about a locker room, road trips, the teammates on a football team and the attention that came from putting on a jersey seemed to pull me toward trouble.

The Arena Football League, featuring a small fifty-yard field with eight players on each side, had launched in 1987 with four teams. The AFL was fun to watch and located teams in smaller cities that couldn't support NFL franchises, so it expanded quickly in those early years. In 1991 in nearby Orlando, the new Predators team was looking for players to fill its roster. I still loved football, and I couldn't resist the chance to hear the roar of the crowd again. Without hesitation, I signed a contract with the Predators, said goodbye to my young wife and daughter, and moved into an apartment in Orlando.

■ ■ ■

CHAPTER EIGHT

TWO LIVES

*In order to see change on the outside,
there must be change on the inside.*

By 1991, when I signed with the Orlando Predators, I had lost a step or two in the backfield and my knees were hurting most of the time. I was in my early thirties and I understood that my best football days were behind me, but I believed I could still play. I had never wanted to do anything else, never had any other type of job aspiration or experience. Football was it, and I was grateful to the Arena League for handing me another opportunity.

I got settled into the hotel that housed the team in Orlando and tried to focus on being the best Arena running back I could be. And I did have success there—I gained 208 receiving yards for four touchdowns that first season. Unfortunately, though, attending practice and meetings and doing team conditioning weren't the only habits from my old football life that I picked up again. Soon I also fell into the same traps in my social life that had plagued me through my NFL career.

Some of my teammates in Orlando were mixed up with drugs, and apparently two years of clean living had not built up the defenses I needed to resist that temptation. Sherod and my three kids were thirty minutes away in Sanford, and I only had to get high one time to remember the firm grip of cocaine once I gave it entry into my life. I had been clean and doing great when I got to Orlando, and in an instant I was worse off than I was before.

I hated myself for what I was doing. When I would come down from a high, I would be plagued by guilt for damaging the stable life I had constructed and for hurting my young family. I was leading a double life—a family man and a church leader at home and a crack user when I would return to Orlando. My wife didn't have a clue at first, because I worked hard to hide what I was doing from her. I was trying to keep the two extremes of my life under control and far from each other, but I think I knew that my deception would eventually backfire.

In addition to the cocaine, I also started drinking more that spring, and the most dramatic incident during this time came one night in Orlando when I got behind the wheel of a rental car when I was high and I had also had too much to drink. I knew I was driving when I shouldn't have been, and soon I saw a police car directly behind me. I know my mind was impaired that night because I actually made a right turn and the cop kept going straight, so I wasn't really in any danger of being pulled over. But I convinced myself that he was still behind me.

I was completely paranoid, and in my mind I was sure that the cops were going to pull me and give me a Breathalyzer and it was going to be all over the papers—Tony Collins, who was once suspended by the NFL for drug use, was arrested for drunk driving. So I decided it would be better if I got in an accident, because that would draw the attention away from my blood-alcohol level. I was beyond irrational, and my next move didn't make any sense then or later.

I saw a big pond up ahead, and so I drove off the road and aimed the rental car straight into that body of water. I was never really in any danger, and in retrospect it's even kind of comical—I was sitting on top of the car in this pond, yelling for help until the police and the fire department arrived. One part of my plan worked—when the police came they didn't give me a DUI. But what actually happened was much worse. The officers at the scene decided I was suicidal and took me to a mental hospital.

Suddenly, a news report of Tony Collins getting a DUI seemed like a much better alternative to the stories that appeared everywhere from Florida to New England. Tony Collins, former Pro Bowler, tried to commit suicide by driving his car into a lake in Florida. More than twenty years later, when someone wrote a Wikipedia entry about me, that false story was repeated on the Internet. But I never really wanted to kill myself, and I told everyone who would listen that they had it all wrong.

I had to stay the night in that facility with all of these crazy people, and I was so relieved the next morning when my sister came to pick me up. When I got home, I told my wife that I had just been in a freak accident, but I told my mom the truth —that I had relapsed and was back into drugs and alcohol.

My mom encouraged me to get back into church, and I was so ashamed that I started going even more often. It wasn't unusual for me to attend church twice a day, and I even served on the usher board. Even while I was using drugs and drinking on the side, I was still a leader in my church's recovery program for addicts. I looked like I had it all together, but that period of relapse had set me on a bad course.

I had played well enough for the Predators in 1991 to be asked to return for a second season, but the Cincinnati Rockers came calling with an opportunity to make more money. I was attracted by the prospect of a bigger paycheck, and it's always nice to be wooed away, but the truth is I never should have left Florida for Ohio. I needed to be as close to home as possible or what little stability I had was going to collapse.

But I wasn't known for making wise decisions in those days, so I boarded a plane for Cincinnati in the winter of 1992. Once I got settled there, it was off to the races again. I told myself that I wasn't too bad off with my cocaine use, because I wasn't going on those crack sprees that lasted two or three days. But during that time I was probably getting high two or three times a week. It was like I was sliding down a muddy mountainside, gaining speed, heading for the same pit that had brought me near death four years earlier, and I didn't have any strong trees or rocks—like my family—nearby to grab. There was nothing in Cincinnati to stop me from destroying myself again.

I became good friends with the Rockers' starting quarterback, a former Ohio State player named Art Schlichter. Art had a different kind of addiction—compulsive gambling—and he and I liked to party together. I thought Art was a little crazy—I couldn't believe that he would resort to criminal activity like writing bad checks just so that he could gamble. But he thought my dependency on cocaine was crazy, too.

Art would have made a great NFL quarterback if he hadn't gotten into so much trouble, and later in life he continued to struggle to kick his addiction. He has said in interviews that he stole $1.5 million over the years and served time in forty-four different prisons and jails, and he was still facing legal trouble as late as 2012, when he tested positive for, of all things, cocaine while serving house arrest for charges on a multimillion dollar ticket scam.

With Art and I helping to make things happen on offense, the Rockers made the playoffs and finished 7-3 that season. When we wrapped up the season and I moved home to Florida, my knees were hurting all the time and I had to have both of them scoped. To help combat the daily pain, I fell back into the habit of taking pain pills, then smoking marijuana, which led to cocaine. It was the first time I had used cocaine regularly in Sanford, which had previously been the location of the 'good' side of my double life.

Suddenly, the dividing wall between my two selves was dissolving. I would be gone for two or three days at a time, and my kids would be asking Sherod, "Where's Dad?" I always had an excuse for her, and I think she wanted to believe that I was doing OK, but the evidence of my backsliding into the drug world was becoming overwhelming.

And it wasn't just the drugs that had reappeared in my life. I was back to the point where I had to have at least one woman with me, and sometimes two or three. There I was in the town where I was an usher and a recovery ministry leader, and suddenly I was in over my head. I felt like I had to have drugs and women with me all the time, and I'm not talking about my wife.

It all came to a head one weekend when I disappeared for a couple of days and I didn't contact Sherod at all. No one close to me had any idea where I was, and my wife was worried and upset. Meanwhile, I was in a hotel room with a random woman I had found somewhere, having a good time.

To this day I'm not sure how my wife found me at that hotel—I guess she saw my car in the parking lot or someone else did—but she located the hotel and got the front desk to tell her which room I was in. It was a very bad scene.

She knocked on the door, and I wouldn't let her in. I just couldn't face her finding me there under those circumstances. She was crying and upset, but eventually she left.

It's hard to believe, but Sherod forgave me for that terrible night. I told her that I would stop partying and sleeping around, that I would stay clean. And I was determined to keep that promise. After that incident in September, I returned to my role of churchgoing family man for five months, until February rolled around and a different Arena team came calling.

When the Miami Hooters offered me a contract for the 1993 season, I should have said, "Thanks, but no thanks." Sherod had a good job and we had enough money to get by, so I couldn't lean on that excuse. And of course, I was smart enough to see a destructive pattern tied directly to my last two stops in the AFL. But even with the harm I had done to my family and myself through my return to football, I was still drawn to the game. I had first become obsessed with football as a young boy, and the temptation to play again was still too strong for me to resist. I told myself that Miami would be my last go-round, and I packed my bags for South Florida.

It didn't take long in Miami for me to realize that it was the worst possible city for me. Miami was the cocaine capital of the world, and beautiful women were everywhere. There was temptation around every corner, and I didn't even trust myself. I had kept my promise to my wife for the first month or two of my season with the Hooters, but soon my resistance grew weak. My kids were finishing out the school year soon, and I came up with an ingenious solution. My seven-year-old son Conredge would come live with me in Miami.

I figured that if my little boy was sleeping in my hotel room I would have to behave. So he moved down to Miami and for a few weekends we had a great time together. We went to Hooters every day for lunch—they gave the players free food because they sponsored the team—and Conredge always ordered a hamburger, every single day. He would stay in the hotel room while I went to practice, and when I returned we would play with a beach ball in the room or go for a dip in the hotel pool.

Before long, though, Conredge got homesick, and so I drove him back to Sanford. Finishing the season in Miami alone was playing with fire, and I knew it. But at that point, football wasn't the only thing keeping me in that city. I had met another woman.

I met Debbie at Hooters, and I was immediately drawn to her. She was very beautiful. First we just talked on the phone a lot, and then I started going over there to see her. I would even bring my son to her house, and I think he kind of knew what was going on. Debbie had a baby, and she had a rocky relationship with the baby's father. We became very attached to each other, and before long we were completely involved.

I didn't exactly set the world on fire as a Miami Hooter—I caught 17 passes for 173 yards and only totaled three rushing yards—and we finished the season 5-7 and out of playoff contention. After our final game, I returned to Sanford, but I had slid so far down from my stable place that it didn't feel like I was going to find my way back this time.

Back home, it didn't take long for me to start disappearing again, and then I really sank to a new low. I started messing around with a married woman in our church. She and I would sneak off to a hotel, do drugs and stay all night together. One of those nights, my wife couldn't find me and her husband couldn't find her, and they put two and two together. My wife extended me grace when I was caught misbehaving at a hotel one time, but I had reached the end of her supply of second chances. We didn't separate right away, but that was the night our marriage was really finished.

That was a low time for me, because I was making one bad choice after another, I knew my football career was probably over and, worst of all for me, that was the year I lost my father. He was eighty-three years old when he died of cancer, and he was a great example of a life well-lived. But I was filled with regret in the midst of my grief, mostly because I knew he had been worried and saddened by what my life had become.

I couldn't even mourn my father without being haunted by my compulsive womanizing. Debbie decided to come up from Miami for the funeral, and she came to my house where Sherod and my kids were. I rode with Sherod in the funeral and sat with her during the service, but Debbie and the other woman from church were also in attendance. Three women I had been trying to have relationships with, all sitting in the same church at my own father's funeral. That's a pretty good snapshot of the mess I was in back then.

After my dad passed away, I officially separated from Sherod—she took Alicia and my older kids and I moved in with my mom. I must have worried my mother to death—I took to disappearing regularly for a day or two, consumed with cocaine and women. My kids would constantly ask, "Where's Dad?" and the thing that got me was the way they would react when I finally came back home. They would jump on me and squeeze me real tight. I was failing them as a father almost daily, and they still loved me unconditionally. I remember Colette saying, "Dad, don't leave anymore."

I am convinced that positive thinking has the power to change a person's life, but the same is true of negative thinking. I still had plenty to be thankful for, but I was plagued by negative thoughts. I would start thinking about getting high, and before long I could taste the drugs in my mouth. Once I started tasting those drugs, I just had to go find some cocaine. My mom was trying to get me to stop, but I was in the grip of that addiction again and I wouldn't even listen to the ones who loved me the most.

My mom talked to my brother Moose, who was living with his wife and kids in a nice house in Rochester, New York, and Moose said that we could come up there and live with him. I didn't really want to leave Florida, but Mom kept telling me it was the best thing for my kids, so finally I relented and packed up for the long trip north.

In New York, we enrolled the kids in school and Conredge, who was nine years old, played on his first real football team. He reminded me a lot of myself at that age—fixated on the game and thrilled to be suiting up for the first time. He played defensive end and he was running all over the field. I was so glad to be there watching him, because I remembered that my dad had not been able to attend my first game. It was the beginning of a new stage for me, as a football father.

Even though the move brought some positive changes for my children, I didn't really like living with my brother. I had become unaccustomed to the cold and I took a thankless job doing asbestos removal. It was also hard to party like I wanted to in a new town without any connections and under my brother's watchful eye. I was still in touch with Debbie down in Miami, and whenever we talked she would try to convince me to move back to Florida.

We had only been in Rochester for a few months, and I was already thinking of leaving. I told my brothers what I was considering and they were dead set against it, I'm sure because they knew I was headed for more trouble down south. But I made my decision, and Debbie drove all the way up to Rochester to pick us up. My family gave me a going-away party, and the next day we turned south to make a life in Miami.

I'm sure my brothers watched us drive away and thought they were losing me for good. I had already learned that Miami isn't exactly the best destination for someone with a drug problem. But I surprised everybody by settling into another pattern of stability when I moved in with Debbie. She had a good job at the post office, and I found a job selling appliances. It turned out I was well suited for sales—I enjoyed talking to people on the floor and I liked the challenge of moving products and earning commission. We were settled in a nice apartment, and we even found a church we loved.

My new family life was so satisfying that I decided Debbie and I should get married. Believe it or not, I had still not taken any steps to get divorced from Sam, who was in North Carolina, or from Sherod. But no one in the state of Florida tried to stop me, so in 1994 I married my third wife, and I guess I was technically a polygamist at that point.

Debbie had a daughter before we got together, and Colette and Conredge were with us. About a year after we got married we found out she was pregnant, and we had another daughter, my namesake, Toni. Shortly after our family grew to six, we moved into a house, where we stayed for nearly ten years. On the surface, our life was smooth. I was still making good money at the appliance store, Conredge was turning heads as a young high school football player and we were in church every Sunday. I even started working as a volunteer youth minister. I was the ideal family man again, making responsible choices and looking out for my wife and kids.

That perfect image was in jeopardy, though, because a guy at work started offering me cocaine. I justified it because when we would step into the back room for a snort of coke, I would have an unbelievable boost of energy, and I would go out and sell like crazy. I could work for ten hours with no lunch break, and I was incredibly productive. But those little snorts were awakening my addiction and setting me on another destructive course.

It was like Sanford all over again—I started partying more, disappearing from home, making up excuses when my kids would ask me where I was. Of course, they were teenagers at this point, and they were wise to what was really happening. But they still loved me and supported me, even when the only thing I really deserved was their rejection.

My daughter Colette left for college at Florida Atlantic, and things continued to go south in my marriage to Debbie. We had differences of opinions about some of the rules laid out by the minister at our church; she wanted to abide by everything he said and I was starting to feel restricted by his limits. More and more, I was seeing lots of other women and keeping it secret from my wife. Finally, when Conredge was about to start his senior year in high school and Colette had spent a year in college, I moved out of Debbie's house after eleven years of marriage and moved in with my nephew.

I still had my job, but living with my nephew was a step in the wrong direction for me. I knew that he both used and sold drugs, so the way I saw it I was in great shape because I could get all the drugs I wanted. Apart my wife, I could also indulge my womanizing habit more frequently.

When I look back, I realize that I was getting most of my significance from my son at that time. My personal football career was over, but I was consumed by my son's talent and the attention he was getting from colleges. I didn't go back to Penn Yan or to Greenville, because I was ashamed at how my NFL career had ended. None of the guys I had played with knew where I was. Instead of looking back on my career, I was soaking up every bit of Conredge's recruitment, even helping to coach the running backs at his high school.

Through Conredge, I hoped to see a career that mirrored mine. I couldn't wait to watch him excel in college and follow my footsteps into the NFL. I spent hours researching colleges, sending information about him out to coaches and helping him navigate the recruiting process. My third marriage had dissolved and I was still plagued by my desire for drugs and women. The one good thing I had, as I saw it, was a son who played football, so I resolved to do whatever it took to help him succeed.

• • •

CHAPTER NINE
A NEW BEGINNING

The choices we make today determine our tomorrow.

When my third marriage broke up and I moved in with my nephew in 2004, it felt like I had been running in place for more than two decades. It had been some twenty-five years since I had started chasing women as a college student and nineteen years since I was introduced to cocaine as an NFL player. I had spent those years—more than half of my lifetime—navigating the peaks, plateaus and valleys of addiction.

But even though I had stayed clean for long stretches of five years or more, drugs and women were always lurking in the background, always waiting for a moment of weakness or a persuasive friend to give them full reign in my life again. I didn't even have my kids around to keep me grounded anymore—Colette was in her third year at Florida Atlantic and Conredge had accepted a scholarship to play in the backfield for Pittsburgh—so I was poised for another downward spiral.

I was back on the edge of the drug culture, unattached, with the son whose football career had consumed me more than a thousand miles away. It would have been a recipe for disaster if God had not sent me a rescuer—an incredible woman who would finally help me cut the ties with those stubborn addictions that had plagued me for so long.

I had lost my job at the appliance store just a few months earlier. To pay the bills, I worked a series of odd jobs, until my cousin went out on a limb to help me get a temporary job with an organization called Lead America. I thought I was going to be able to work with kids, to travel around to universities and help with the company's leadership programs, but when I got there the first day I found out that I was hired to make telephone calls.

There I sat at a desk, on the phone all day talking to parents of prospective college students, and I was extremely frustrated. I was thinking that I would rather work at McDonald's than do this job, and I remember thinking, "When I go to lunch, I'm not coming back." But then I thought about my cousin, who had stuck her neck out for me, and I realized I couldn't ditch the job before my first day was even over. So I went back to my cubicle that afternoon and finished out the day.

I didn't want to, but because I knew it was the right thing to do I went back to Lead America for my second day of work too, and that decision changed my life. The phone on the desk next to me rang, but I picked it up because that person had stepped away, and on the other end was a lady from San Antonio named Trudy Navarre.

Trudy was trying to get money back because she had overpaid the company, and she needed some details about the refund process. I started taking down her son's information, and when she told me his name was Terrence Terrell I said, "That sounds like a football name." She told me that her son did play football, and pretty soon we were having a conversation about our sons and their success on the gridiron.

I didn't want to stop talking to her, but I wasn't even on my own phone. For some reason, I told her to call me back in about an hour on my extension. We talked some more and looked up information about each other's sons on the computer. When it was time for me to leave work, I said, "Why don't you call me on my cellphone?"

I really didn't think she was going to call me again, but that evening the phone rang, and it was Trudy. We talked for hours, and then we talked for hours every day from that day forward. We used to talk so long that I would fall asleep on the phone with her. We told each other a lot of things about our lives, and I learned that Trudy had high standards and expected people to take responsibility for their lives. She had been through a bad scene with her ex-husband, and I was pretty sure that she would be done with me when she learned the ugly details of my past.

Of course, my missteps over the years hadn't exactly been secrets. A quick Internet search told Trudy everything she needed to know about the NFL suspension, the drug use, even the suicide attempt that didn't really occur. Despite all of that, she must have seen something in me that I didn't even see in myself, because before I knew it she was making plans to visit me in Miami.

As her visit approached, I was so nervous. I still hadn't seen her at all, except for a black and white picture she had sent me that was about twenty years old. The truth was, I knew she was different from any other woman I had ever known, and I was sure that I wanted to be with her. I remember my daughter Colette saying, "Dad, what if she's ugly? What are you going to do?" And I said, "I don't know, but I'm in love with her."

In fact, Trudy was beautiful, and the more time I spent with her the more I started to see things differently. She was so encouraging. One example was the way I had started to view Penn Yan and East Carolina—the places that had handed me so many opportunities in my youth. The deeper I had fallen into the pit of addiction and bad choices, the more separation I had put between myself and those good memories. I stayed away, avoiding every reunion, every homecoming game, every phone call from an old teammate trying to catch up. When Trudy heard about that pattern, she said, "You should go back home. Those people there still love you." Before long, I would discover that she was right.

Over and over, I wondered why Trudy was bothering with me. I was the picture of instability—suspended driver's license, terrible credit and no bank account. Trudy was the complete opposite. She had her own home, a steady job and money in the bank. But incredibly, she wanted to be with me. I can't even tell you how much that encouraged me, that she could see through so much garbage to my heart and see goodness there. Her love was so strong that it started to restore me.

It was like God sent me an incredible Hail Mary pass play in the last seconds of the fourth quarter, when I seemed guaranteed to lose the game. With Conredge off at school, I didn't care about anything anymore. I didn't want anyone to know who I was and I didn't really care about anything. I was depressed, and I couldn't muster up the energy to make anything better in my life. I can't even imagine where I would be if I hadn't gone back to that job that day and answered my phone.

We had such a great time on that visit that I didn't want her to go back to Texas. When she finally had to leave, we made plans for me to visit her in August for her birthday.

But when I made the trip to San Antonio in August, I never went back to Miami. I was leaving behind the bad influences and destructive patterns that had dragged me down for the woman who believed I could stand tall.

Down in Texas, Trudy started helping me untangle the mess I had made of my life. My driver's license had been suspended three years earlier in Florida, and I had been driving around illegally all that time, but things were different with Trudy. She was a stickler for the rules and for doing things the right way, so she pushed me to go to the DMV so that I could get a valid Texas license. But what started as an innocent driver's license application turned into the first major trial Trudy and I would face together.

When the DMV employee pulled me up on the computer that day, it said that there was a warrant for my arrest in Florida. I had no idea what it was all about—it turned out that my nephew had been charged with possession and the cops were charging me with child neglect, because my son had been living there when the drugs were found.

Trudy had dropped me off at the DMV, and when she came back to pick me up she found me in the back room, stunned at what was happening. They told me I had to go to the police station to straighten out the situation. The officer there told me that I had an outstanding warrant and that I had to go back to Miami to face the charges.

It was almost Thanksgiving by the time I found out about the warrant, and I expected that I would be able to fly back to Miami and get the problem taken care of quickly, hopefully in time to spend most of the holidays back in Texas with Trudy. It was so hard to leave, because I had already gotten very close to her five-year-old daughter Taylor, whose father had never been around. On the first day I met Taylor she had said, "Can I call you Dad?" And now, against my will, I was leaving her too.

My hopes for a quick flight and easy resolution to the warrant turned out to be pipe dreams. I did not board a plane for Miami, but instead I got in a van full of other prisoners who had to be extradited to other states. What followed was one of the biggest nightmares of my life. That van drove all over the country for three and a half days, going to Fargo, North Dakota, then to New York City, then finally down to Florida.

I had been through quite a bit at that point, with my misdeeds splashed on ESPN, but that trip was easily the most embarrassing thing I have ever endured. I had to wear an orange jumpsuit with chains around my waist, and every time we stopped to go to the bathroom people stared at us like we were terrifying criminals. We got two hamburgers a day to eat and water to drink, and we weren't permitted to shower or even brush our teeth. It felt like I was never going to get out of that van.

I finally finished the road trip from hell and faced the authorities in Miami, but things didn't get much better there. I had a missed a court date that I didn't even know about, because I had spontaneously moved to Texas and had not been in contact with my nephew. It started to dawn on me that I was in more trouble than I thought and that straightening things out might take a while.

They put me in jail while I waited for my day in court, and I remember thinking that this was certainly the end of my young relationship with Trudy. Because of my arrest, she was learning even more disturbing details about my past behavior, and there was no telling when I was going to be free to live a normal life with her. I was so in love with her, and I remember thinking, "I'm not going to put her through this." Right after I got to Miami, I called her and said, "I understand if you want to be done with me. Whatever you decide to do, I completely understand."

But even though I didn't have much hope, I wanted so badly for her to stick with me. I remember sitting in my little cell, praying to God, telling Him, "I truly believe that you brought Trudy to me, and if it's your will that we stay together then I believe that we will. I'm just leaving it in your hands."

I got my answer just two days after I arrived in Miami, when I learned that Trudy had hired a very good lawyer for me. She wouldn't tell me how much she had to pay him, but she was always encouraging when we talked, reassuring me that the lawyer was going to get the charges dropped. The lawyer was from Fort Lauderdale, and after a few days they moved me to the Broward County Jail in that city. I ended up staying in jail for five weeks, through Thanksgiving and Christmas.

Soon after I got to Fort Lauderdale, I met with the lawyer and he reviewed my case. He said that if my nephew just came to court and testified that the marijuana was his I should be cleared. But things were completely messed up because I had missed my court date, so miserable weeks passed while I waited for them to get me in front of a judge.

My time in jail was truly horrible, and even more so because I really had not done anything to warrant giving more than a month of my life to the Florida correctional system. But even though each day was a trial, I was happy during those weeks because it had started to dawn on me that Trudy really was going to stay by my side. We were talking and writing to each other, and she was telling me that she wouldn't give up on me, and I knew that she was giving her time and money every day to get me out of there.

I know for a fact that Trudy had a $2,000 phone bill during that period, and I found out later that she paid the lawyer $11,000 out of her own savings. If that doesn't illustrate the miracle she was in my life, I don't know what does. It would have been so easy for her to walk away when that warrant surfaced, and what she did makes no sense at all except through the lens of love. Imagine what her friends thought: "You mean you just met this guy, you've known him for six months, he's a cocaine addict, and now you're going to pay $11,000 to get him out of jail?"

I remembered clearly my father telling me that everything happens for a reason, so I started looking for other inmates who needed encouragement, and I went to Bible study in the jail twice a week. When the other guys heard that I had played in the NFL, they gathered around to hear what I had to say, so I had this great platform to share my past struggles and the gifts God had given me. Even from jail, I was starting to see that God had protected me and had mapped out a bright future beyond those prison walls.

When I was doing time, I believe that God planted the first seeds of what would become a mission to help other people. I met men who had committed truly horrible crimes, like child molestation or armed robbery. These guys knew that they would be in for at least twenty years, so they were often ready to listen to words of hope. That was really encouraging for me, because it showed me that I could be used for good in other people's lives. I realized, in those long hours of thought and prayer in my cell, that more than anything I wanted to help kids so that they could avoid falling into the traps that had ensnared me.

I welcomed 2006 behind bars, but finally in mid-January I got a court date and everything went exactly as my lawyer had hoped. The judge cleared me of all charges and my daughter picked me up and drove me to the airport, where Trudy had booked a flight back to San Antonio that very afternoon. I was heading for a different life. I was free, and I was determined to stay that way.

In Texas, I found a job at another appliance store, and even though I liked the work I had bigger dreams—dreams that for the first time had nothing to do with football. I talked to Trudy for hours about my desire to help people, to use my negative experiences for good. I had a great relationship with Trudy's kids – her daughter Taylor was little, her older daughter Terrie was out of college and her son TJ was about to finish high school when I moved there. Trudy was supportive of my dreams, and as TJ prepared to go to college she had an idea that meant yet another sacrifice for her.

Trudy thought that we should move out of San Antonio to a place where I would have more opportunities to serve others and tell my story. She worked for Wells Fargo Bank and figured she could get a job anywhere, and she was determined to find a place where I could thrive. Everything about that decision was sacrificial, because the truth is she loved San Antonio and was very comfortable with her life there. But we decided together that we should be closer to my family and to people who knew me, so we made plans to move back to Sanford, Florida.

My mom had passed away seven years before, and being back in Sanford made me miss my parents more than I can express. But I still had brothers and sisters and nieces and nephews there, and we got a two-bedroom apartment until we could get stable enough to buy a house. I was still on probation from the earlier charges but I wasn't doing anything I shouldn't, and I found a job I loved working at a fitness center.

But incredibly, there was still one more bump in the road for me, and it soured our view of living in Florida. I had met with my probation officer when I arrived there and he told me I needed a Florida driver's license. One day I was driving the five minutes home from work when I saw him in the parking lot looking at me. He followed me, but he didn't confront me at all. At my next appointment, though, I realized something was up.

When I arrived at his office, he called in a policeman in who told me I had violated my probation because I had a Texas driver's license. Before I knew what was happening, they had taken me back to Fort Lauderdale and I was back in jail. I stayed there for more than two weeks that time, and it was really a misunderstanding, because the authorities thought I had been driving on an expired license. The judge was a stickler who wouldn't listen to anything I said, so she made me serve more time while they sorted it out, but when my lawyer finally showed that the Texas license was valid they let me go.

Trudy's son TJ had accepted a football scholarship to Nicholls State in Louisiana, but he wasn't getting much playing time and he was unhappy there. I contacted Skip Holtz, the head coach at East Carolina, to see if they might give him a shot at my alma mater. Coach Holtz offered to let TJ walk on and get a scholarship if he did well, which opened a door to ECU that I had kept closed for twenty-five years.

We still weren't sure that Sanford was the place to build our life together, and Trudy had the thought that we should consider following TJ to Greenville, especially because I wanted to finally finish my college degree and we felt like I might have a shot at getting a job at ECU. We made a few calls and decided North Carolina was the place where we should settle, so just a few months after moving to Florida we were packing again.

I was going back to the place that had welcomed me as an innocent eighteen-year-old with huge football dreams. This time, I had walked through countless dark valleys and I had left a trail of broken relationships and missed opportunities. But because of Trudy's love and belief in me, I was confident that I could rebuild my life in Greenville, that I could become someone that my family and friends could be proud of. The first step in that process was going back to college.

. . .

CHAPTER TEN
NO REGRETS

Live life to the fullest.

Before we moved back to Greenville, North Carolina in the winter of 2006, I had flown up there for a meeting with ECU athletic director Terry Holland, and he was very encouraging about the prospect of a job for me in the athletic department. It wasn't official, but it seemed like the right people were determined to make it happen, so I enrolled in school for the fall semester and my family and I moved into our new home.

After my meeting with Holland, ECU had run a background check on me, and shortly after I arrived in Greenville I learned that there was a major problem because of my child neglect charge in Florida. Everyone at ECU was really nice, but they all told me the same thing—there was no way they could hire me with that charge on my record. It was frustrating, because I so badly wanted to rebuild my life.

I might not have been employed, but I was a part-time college student, and so I focused on finding the discipline to succeed in college as a forty-eight-year-old man. Because I had been planning on working at ECU during the day, I had enrolled in two online classes, but I quickly realized that

Internet courses were not for me. I remember taking online tests that were on a timer, and even though they were open book tests I felt so much pressure that I was just dripping sweat, and I still didn't answer all the questions. For the rest of my semesters, I switched to real classes with a room and a live professor, which suited my learning style much better.

Looking back, I realize that losing the ECU job was a blessing in disguise. That fall, Trudy convinced me to renew my ties with the NFL, the league that had handed me my dream and, as I had once seen it, snatched it away. I had harbored bitterness toward the men who suspended me for years, but I had matured enough by then to understand that my troubles were actually due to my own bad choices. So, at Trudy's urging, I filled out a little card with my information and sent it back to the NFL so that I could join the NFL Player's Association.

Just a few weeks after I joined, I received an e-mail from the NFLPA passing on an opportunity to former players. A high school recruiting organization called NCSA was looking for ex-athletes to join its speakers network. The NCSA speakers travel around the country meeting with athletes who are hoping to earn an athletic scholarship and speaking to them about successfully navigating the recruiting process.

I had been searching for a way to help kids, and I had always wanted to try public speaking, so I contacted NCSA. They asked me if I could get myself to Chicago for an interview, so Trudy made the arrangements and I flew up there to learn more about the job.

On that visit, I realized that NCSA really was the perfect job for me. It was flexible, I got to travel and I never had to sit in an office, I made good money and, best of all, I was helping young people who had the same dream that had driven me as a child. Six years after signing a contract, I was still loving my job with NCSA and growing every time I got to speak.

My stepson TJ never really got a chance to shine at ECU, in part because he blew out his knee during his time there and he was playing behind superstar Dwayne Harris. But TJ did thrive academically, graduating on time and then pursuing a master's degree.

Meanwhile, up at Pittsburgh, my son Conredge had been pursuing his own football dream. Conredge was the starting fullback for the Panthers for three seasons, and at then end of his senior year he was considered one of the best fullback prospects for the 2009 draft. He was hearing encouraging things from scouts, but his draft status wasn't a lock, and we had a major difference of opinion about where he should spend draft day.

The NFL draft just happened to fall on the same day as his college graduation, and I was prepared for my trip to Pittsburgh to celebrate that major milestone. I believed that there was nothing more important for Conredge than to walk across that stage and accept his diploma. But he wanted to have a big draft party down in Miami—to gather lots of friends together to hear some team executive call his name on ESPN.

I lost that battle, and Conredge planned his party. Quite a few of my family members joined him in Miami that day, but I scheduled an NCSA event in Boston. I had never forgotten my collegiate teammate who threw a big party and then went undrafted, and above all I thought my family needed to be celebrating in Pittsburgh that weekend.

My worst fears were realized that Saturday when Conredge didn't get drafted at all. It broke my heart for him, but he got better news a few days later when Tampa Bay picked him up as a free agent. Unfortunately, the rollercoaster ride continued when he broke his foot on the second day of minicamp, and that was the beginning of a long medical nightmare.

About a month after his injury, Conredge called me and told me that his foot was throbbing and he was in severe pain. I begged him to come up to live in North Carolina with me through his recovery so that we could take care of him, but he wanted to stay down in Miami. I convinced him to go to the doctor, and when he got there he found out he had a serious staph infection in his foot, and if he had waited another week they would have had to amputate. They had to take out the hardware and clean up the infection, and then he had to have an IV and a home health nurse at his apartment. At that point, he knew he had lost a year of football.

Even after a year, Conredge still couldn't walk properly on that foot, and he was overweight and out of shape. It was a really rough time for him, and he wanted to navigate those trials his own way without my guidance. I just tried to love him and remind him that there is a reason for everything we go through. Three years after that injury, he was rehabbing and still hoping for another shot at the NFL.

When we were living in Florida, we made plans to get married and even went to the courthouse. But when we arrived we were stopped by the news that my marriage to Debbie had never legally ended. Trudy, always by the book, insisted that I take care of that little problem, but it wasn't easy. We had a hard time serving the papers on Debbie because she didn't want get divorced; she kept dodging the people who came to her house with the papers. Finally she signed, and in April of 2008, we finally got married in a small ceremony at the courthouse in Greenville. Our plan is to have a giant wedding ceremony on the tenth anniversary of that 'official' wedding, in 2018.

Every step of the way, from the day I met her on that random telephone call, Trudy has literally been a lifesaver, not just for me but for my entire family. My kids have learned so much from her, and she has provided the stability that they craved in their early years. They have told me, "We love you Dad, but we're on Trudy's side. If you ever do her wrong, you're on your own."

They don't need to worry. I know a gift when I see one, and Trudy has been an extravagant, undeserved gift from God sent to show me how life was meant to be lived. She tells me time and again that I deserve the credit for turning my life around, that I am responsible for making the good choices that led to brighter days. But I know with certainty that she is the one who put my feet on that path, and a few times in those early months she gave of her money, her time and her heart to grab me and forcibly turn me back in the right direction when the trials seemed too hard to face.

One of the many positive steps that Trudy urged me to take was my return to ECU for my degree. I had squandered my first chance at graduating from college, and I had no intention of repeating that mistake. But even though I was determined, there were times it seemed like a mountain climb. Because of my earlier academic struggles, I couldn't make anything lower than a C or I would have been kicked out of school, so for the first time in my life I really had to learn to study and stay on top of assignments.

It wasn't just the academic pressure that presented a challenge for me; my knees were hurting so bad by the time I returned to school that I could hardly walk to class. I learned the location of every elevator on the ECU campus, because climbing stairs was out of the question. But when I got there, knees throbbing, I encountered professors like Dr. K in the communications department, gifted teachers who made me grateful for the opportunity to learn. I was a little late to that realization, which is one of the reasons I love to remind kids that they should regard education as a precious commodity.

I had to work incredibly hard for every grade, but finally, in the spring of 2011, I walked across that stage as a college graduate at the age of fifty-two. All of my kids flew in from Florida, New York and Virginia to watch me graduate. It was such an amazing day, and I was so glad that they could be proud of my example when I had spent large parts of their childhood demonstrating what not to do. The perseverance and dedication it took to earn that diploma has helped remind me—in the second half of my life—that I can face any challenge head-on.

2011 was a pretty significant year for me. Just a few months after my graduation, I was notified that I had been selected for induction into the ECU Athletics Hall of Fame. It was a huge honor, and it became another big event for the Collins family. My brothers came down from New York, and my kids were there for the ceremony, which was held at halftime of the ECU homecoming game.

I was so grateful to be inducted into the Hall of Fame of the university that had given me so many opportunities, and the year after that I learned that I had been selected for the Penn Yan Academy Hall of Fame as well. But when I remember the ECU honor, I remember more than the remarks, the crowd in the stadium or the plaque they handed me. I remember that my knees hurt so bad that I had to walk down the steps to the football field sideways, and standing up through the ceremony was excruciating.

Fortunately, a month after the Hall of Fame awards, I went to the hospital to have my right knee replaced. Exactly a week later, I had the same procedure done on my left knee. The orthopedist told me that my right knee was the worst one he had ever seen. For years I had been hobbling around like an old man, but I never took anything stronger than Aleve or an occasional cortisone shot. I knew that I had an addictive personality and that stronger painkillers could undo all of the progress I had made in my battle against drugs.

Even in the days right after the surgery, when everyone talked about how much pain I would feel and the doctor had handed us a prescription for pain pills, I hardly took them at all. I took a few pills so that I could sleep, but Trudy and I agreed that I needed to get off of them fast. And I had been in so much pain before the surgeries that the discomfort during rehabilitation was really not too bad for me.

I feel like a new man now. I can play eighteen holes of golf, and I don't have to use a cart unless I want to. I can go to the mall or the grocery store with my wife. I can help lead football clinics, and I even did a little Zumba at an event promoting my 2012 golf tournament in Penn Yan. Thanks to Trudy's encouragement, my clean lifestyle and my new knees, my life has really taken off. I love my job, and anytime someone offers me an opportunity to speak about my story, I jump at the chance. I truly believe that nothing is wasted in God's economy, and He intends for me to use the struggles of my life to help others make better choices.

The Bible talks about the peace that passes all understanding, and I can say without hesitation that I have found the peace that always eluded me before. In the first couple of years after I met Trudy and turned things around, those negative thoughts would still come back occasionally, the ideas about doing drugs or running around with women. But I truly don't focus on those old habits at all anymore. I have no desire to do the things that once gave my life meaning, because I have found my peace and purpose in God, my family and my work.

Even when I was destroying my NFL career and my early marriages, I always understood that there was power in my thoughts. As a young boy, lying awake in bed and visualizing myself in an NFL stadium, I believed that I could make it happen if I worked hard and stayed focused. Even in the depths of my addiction and my hopelessness, I understood that the thoughts of crack and womanizing were leading me down into that valley. If there is a Bible verse that sums up the changes in me, it is Romans 12:2, which says, "Do not conform to the pattern of this world, but be transformed by the renewing of your mind." Today I am operating with a renewed mind, and it has changed the way I see everything.

I am always eager to help young people, but another group of people I hope to encourage is former NFL players like me, men who might be drowning in hopelessness and the aftereffects of a career in such an intense sport. My heart hurts every time I hear about a former great who succumbed to addiction or depression because they couldn't figure out how to navigate life after football. One such tragedy, in May of 2012, was the suicide of Junior Seau.

Junior was an unbelievable football player—he made the Pro Bowl 10 times during his years with the Chargers—and also a good man. He loved his community and his family, and there were no indications that he had a problem with alcohol or drugs. In fact, the autopsy showed no illegal substances in his system, and the report didn't cite brain injury from concussion as a contributing cause of his suicide. Of course, Junior took plenty of hard hits in his nineteen-year career, so the autopsy report didn't stop the rampant speculation that his despair—when everything in his life seemed to be going well —was linked to the fast and furious way he played the game.

We will likely never understand why Junior Seau chose to shoot himself that morning in California, but I do understand the culture of the NFL that led him to play through pain and take hard hits without complaint. He entered the league just two years after I left, and I know that the job required an uncompromising toughness that, in Junior's case, earned plenty of admiration when he was racking up tackles. It also could have contributed to his death. Sports Illustrated writer Peter King considered the positive reinforcement that fans and the media gave players like Seau, and he concluded that the public only harms athletes by glorifying rough play.

"I don't know what happened to Junior Seau," King wrote shortly after Seau's death. "But I do know it bothers me that I helped create this image of a man incapable of feeling what you and I feel. In the end he must have felt more pain than any of us could imagine. And for that reason I know I'll be a lot more cautious about praising men as heroes for playing with injuries they shouldn't be playing with."

King's honest words were a reminder of my early years in the NFL, when even serious injuries were annoyances to be pushed aside with an unhealthy reliance on painkillers. The trainers who gave me those pills weren't trying to start me on a path that led to a destructive cocaine addiction; they were merely acting within the culture that paid their salaries. But in the end, that 'play at all costs' mentality nearly cost me my life.

I wish Junior Seau's story were isolated. From 2009 to 2012, more than a dozen retired professional athletes committed suicide, including former NFL standouts like Dave Duerson, Andre Waters and Ray Easterling. And with the emotional, physical and financial trauma that often accompanies NFL retirement, I fear that Junior is not going to be the last life cut short. I hold onto hope that his death will lead to change in the way the game is played and in the support offered to men on the other side of their playing careers.

"While the physiology of a damaged brain surely plays a role in many cases, it doesn't tell the whole story," wrote Scott Tinley, a retired elite triathlete who has done extensive research into the struggles of retired athletes. "The social and psychological factors in the arc of an athlete's life should not be overlooked. For a person who has been treated as a god-like figure for most of their life, re-entering society without the bright lights is a dark and difficult task."

After Junior's death, there was renewed interest in a series of lawsuits, still pending in late 2012, filed against the NFLPA by at least 2,000 former players, including me. I decided to add my name to the list of those wanting answers because I played football in the years when concussions were routinely swept under the rug. We didn't talk about concussions; we just said we 'got our bells rung' and ran back out onto the field. In recent years, an increase in tragic deaths among young people on the football field and enlightening new medical research has ensured that coaches and trainers will never again ignore a concussion.

That's progress, and my grandsons will have healthier football careers because they are playing in a more educated era. But those of us who endured countless head injuries still believe that the NFL needs to answer for years of neglect.

I know that I suffered several concussions and went out and played again the same day. And while I feel like my mental capacity is normal in my early fifties, I sometimes fear that the effects of all of those tackles will hit me as I get older.

My participation in that lawsuit addresses a certain problem—concussions—but as I have matured and conquered my addictions I have stopped blaming the NFL for the dark and twisted path that was my life for so many years. I own every one of my bad choices, and I have tried diligently to make amends for the relationships I damaged with the wreckage of my drug use and womanizing. Maybe I could have avoided those pitfalls if I had failed to make it the NFL, but I'll never know that for sure.

Above all, I am truly grateful to professional football—to the opportunities it gave a football-crazy young man who had the audacity to dream big. I had some great moments on the football field, and I wouldn't trade one of those game days for anything. It's certainly tempting to wonder what my career would have looked like if I had stayed clean as a player, but these days I'm too busy counting my blessings to waste much time on regret.

Football was a wonderful part of my life, and my standing as an ex-athlete has certainly opened doors for me later in my life. But I save my biggest dose of gratitude for my wife Trudy—who truly demonstrated the power of relentless love to change a life. She was stubborn about pulling me back from the brink, and there were times it was her strong grip alone that held me. Today I can embrace my children and grandchildren, help others with my story and enjoy every day of my life, because I know that even in the darkest valleys God was there, sketching the beautiful picture of my redemption.

· · ·

TONY COLLINS IN
THE NEW ENGLAND PATRIOTS
RECORD BOOK

*1st for most rushing yards in a single game, for 212 yards on 22 attempts against the New York Jets on Sept. 18, 1983

*Tied for 1st for most rushing touchdowns in a game, 3 touchdowns in the same game against the Jets.

*3rd in all-time career rushing with 4,647 yards

*3rd in all-time career rushing attempts with 1,191 attempts

*5th in rushing touchdowns with 32

*6th in total touchdowns, with 44 (32 rushing and 12 receiving)

*10th in career receiving yards with 2,356

*11th in average yards per carry, with 3.9

*11th in all-time scoring

"Tony Collins is the best all-around back in football."
—New England Patriots head coach
Raymond Berry, fall of 1986

QUOTES

Several years ago, I started using Facebook as a platform to encourage others. I am sharing some of those posts here in the hopes that they will remind you of how great life is when we stay positive:

"Every Day is a Good Day." If you have a roof over your head, it's a good day. If you have shoes on your feet, it's a good day. If you have clothes on your back, it's a good day. If you woke up this morning, it's a good day. "Today is a Good Day." STAY POSITIVE! Much love and God bless...

"I will make it." Sometimes you just need to talk to yourself. When there's no one to encourage you, you have to encourage yourself. There's no one who can stop you but you. "You will make it." STAY POSITIVE! Much love and God bless...

"What you think about the most will come to you." Think about it. If you think you can, you will and if you think you can't, you won't. Don't think about what you don't want to happen; think about what you do want to happen. STAY POSITIVE! Much love and God bless...

"It's Possible." When I give, I always receive. When I think positive, I always get positive results. No weapon formed against me shall prosper. God won't allow me to go through anything I can't handle. Whatever I put my mind to, I can accomplish. It doesn't matter how bad it looks, God will always come through for me. God will supply all my needs. I will live a long healthy life. Money will always come to me. I am God's best. "All things are possible when we believe." STAY POSITIVE! Much love and God bless...

"Become What You Believe." You can only become what you believe, so what you think about yourself is very important. "It doesn't matter what anyone else thinks, what matters is what you believe." STAY POSITIVE! Much love and God bless...

"Things will change." It's OK right now if you're going through a little something, because it's gonna change. It doesn't matter how tough it may seem, it's gonna change. Don't focus on the problem, focus on the solution. I believe God allows us to go through things so that we can become stronger and wiser. Not only will your situation change, you will too. STAY POSITIVE! Much love and God bless...

"If I can see it, I can achieve it." There is nothing wrong with dreaming, and it's good to have an imagination, but you have to have a vision. I believe one of the most important things in life is to have a vision of where you're going. "See it, achieve it." STAY POSITIVE! Much love and God bless...

"You are only as good as you think you are." There was a time in my life when I wasn't so positive and I even felt like a loser, but God didn't see me that way. We have to see ourselves as God sees us. The moment I started to see myself as God saw me and began thinking the right way, my life changed. "Don't get caught up in your mistakes, nobody's perfect." STAY POSITIVE! Much love and God bless...

"You still need to forgive." I know some people might say that there are some things that you can't forgive people for, but I believe we have to forgive no matter what the situation is. It's not about the person that did you wrong or what they did; it's about you. You can't hold on to all that bitterness, the only one you're hurting is you. "If we don't forgive, how can we be forgiven?" STAY POSITIVE! Much love and God bless...

"Our words have power." When I was 9 years old I told my mom that I was going to play in the NFL, and I did. When I was in high school my senior year, I said to one of my teammates (Cris Crissy), wouldn't it be cool if we both made it to the NFL? We both got drafted by the New England Patriots in 1981. "Your words have power." STAY POSITIVE! Much love and God bless...

"Be Thankful Today." Every day we wake up is a day to give thanks. You might not be where you want to be in life, but you have another day to work at it. "Today Be Thankful," STAY POSITIVE! Much love and God bless...

"It doesn't matter." It doesn't matter how many times you fall, what matters is that you get up every time. It doesn't matter how bad it may look, what matters is what do you see. It doesn't matter if people talk about you, what matters is what do you think about you. It doesn't matter if you're going through something right now, what matters is that you believe God is bigger than what you're going through. "Doesn't matter." STAY POSITIVE! Much love and God bless...

"Just be thankful." I know sometimes we may feel that life is not fair and say, 'Why do I have to go through this and that?', and we may even find ourselves complaining. This is the time to sit back and see all the good things God has given us. Don't dwell on what we don't have; dwell on what we do have. "Why should God give us more when we are not thankful for what we already have?" STAY POSITIVE! Much love and God bless...

"Live with no regrets." Don't let your past interfere with your future. Stop worrying about what you used to do or who you used to be. You can't change your past but you can surely affect your future. "The only way to get old is that you have to live." STAY POSITIVE! Much love and God bless...

Success begins with being humble and thankful for where you are and what you have. "Increase will come." STAY POSITIVE! Much love and God bless...

ABOUT THE AUTHORS

Tony Collins is still the third-time leading rusher in New England Patriots history. He spent seven seasons in the NFL after a productive career at East Carolina University. He works for NCSA as a recruiting expert partner speaker and he also helps youth through the Tony Collins Foundation, charity golf tournaments and his motivational speaking career, which gives him the chance to share his story all over the country. Tony lives in Greenville, NC with his wife Trudy, and he has nine children and five grandchildren.

Bethany Bradsher has been a journalist since 1990 and a sportswriter since 1995. She has covered the Carolina Panthers, the preparations for the Atlanta Olympics, Wofford College and East Carolina University and she has written articles for dozens of magazines and websites on the regional and national level. "Broken Road" is her third book and her first ghostwriting project. Bethany lives in Greenville, North Carolina with her husband Sid and their four children.

Become What You Believe

The Power of Positive Thinking

Tony is available to share his story with all kinds of groups--youth organizations, non-profits, civic groups, churches or others. To book Tony for your gathering, please contact him at tonycollinsbwyb@yahoo.com.

For more information about Tony's fundraising and community work in the Penn Yan, NY area, visit **www.tonycollinsfoundation.com**.